RELIGION OF TOMORROW

RELIGION
of TOMORROW

JOHN ELOF BOODIN

University of California at Los Angeles

PHILOSOPHICAL LIBRARY

NEW YORK

201
B644

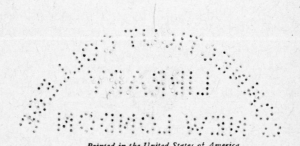

To My Lifelong Friends,

Winifred and Charles Henry Rieber

PREFACE

This book has been written to help thoughtful souls in a time of crisis to understand more clearly and thereby enter more truly into the religious life. It is not addressed to professional philosophers. Indeed the author has derived more help from the poets than the philosophers in preparing these pages. But while the book is not a philosophy of religion in the old specu- lative sense, it does aim to furnish a religious philosophy of life. The hope of the author is above all to awaken a new con- sciousness of the reality of religion and thus to call men to the creative life. If the reader should feel after reading this book that what I call the Religion of Tomorrow is only a new state- ment of the religion of Jesus of Nazareth, I shall feel happy, but I shall still maintain that it is the religion of the future. Vital Religion is always concerned with the future, with the Promise, the fuller meaning of life.

Since this book is addressed to the religious community, the language of popular religion has been used. For a larger cosmic setting, the reader may be referred to the volume on *God,* the Macmillan Company, 1934.

The University Club of Los Angeles
January First, Nineteen Hundred and Forty-Three

CONTENTS

Chapter One

INTRODUCTION

THE FUNCTION OF RELIGION

Religion is the eternal poetry of life. When the human mind awoke on this little planet and began to become conscious of its bent, it discovered a strange disharmony between its inner demands and the environment in which it found itself. And so it set about re-creating the world to make it a fit abode for the spirit of man. It created a new heaven and a new earth in keeping with its dimly conscious ideals. This creative function is ever a vital need of the mind of man. From our striving and ideals it builds out the harmonious completion, defying the gravitation of the world of appearance which would keep us earth-bound. It surrounds this prosy work-a-day life with the sunset halo of infinity.

To meet the apparently indifferent physical environment, it creates a climate in which the spirit can breathe and create. It bids us look beyond the mountains which hem in this little narrow gorge of circumstance and discloses to us, through the rifts of our cloudy ignorance, the vast stretches of the open plains of opportunity. It enhances the prospect by the blue haze of imaginative perspective and thus gives meaning to a life which otherwise would be poor, sordid, and mean. It holds out the apples of the tree of knowledge for those who have the self-control and venturesomeness to seek the truth. It transforms the thorns and thistles of our troubles, through industry and hope, into a garden of human achievement. It makes happiness and content blossom as the rose in what would otherwise be a joyless desert.

Religion and the Building out of Values

Religion thus strives to compensate by its ideal supplemen-
tation for the lack which we feel in the world as it is. The
world of the senses is a panorama of changing things. But in
this world of change we learn to observe certain regularities;
and by dear-bought experience we find that some things are
good for us and some are bad. The human mind, moreover,
insists that somehow this little life of ours and the world of
which we are a part must have meaning. It seeks for harmony
within this dance of circumstance. Its efforts have been crude
enough. It takes a long time to sort and organize such a motley
world of detail. But the instinctive feeling of the human mind
has ever been that the world without can be no less reasonable
than the world within; that intelligence and purpose are somehow to be found within the riddle of things if we can just
penetrate beneath appearances and discover the essential. The
world beyond us must somehow be congenial to this fragment
of it which strives to understand it.

Out of this religious conviction science grows, for science
first germinates within the bosom of religion. It is the offspring
of the religious instinct to seek for meaning in the world. It is
true that science works with severer methods and superior tools
than those of primitive religion. It constructs balances and microscopes and telescopes. It invents a technique of patient research.
It enlarges for us the realm of nature's routine. It increases our
powers of control. For the fairies and nature sprites of primitive
faith it substitutes the mechanical conceptions of causality. It
subjects the imagination to a stern discipline. It would fain
banish poetry from the world. But it ill becomes it to be disloyal to its mother. And the human mind still raises its protest
that the world is more than mechanism, more than chance
ensembles of things. It insists on its faith, though more precisely expressed than that of primitive man, that the laws of

thought are somehow the laws of things, and that a superior reason somehow reveals itself in the working of the whole. Thus religion ekes out the circumscribed world of science and furnishes the inspiration that science itself lives by. For science, though sometimes unwittingly, is still nursed by the life-blood of its mother. The sincere and loyal devotion to truth is a religious devotion and must ever press on to the meaning of the wholeness of things.

It is not enough that we discover unity and meaning in our world, but we demand constant objects of loyalty. This is a world of change. Earth's glories pass away. Love grows cold. The friends we have trusted may fail us in the hour of need. They change or we change, and the harmony fails like "sweet bells jangled out of tune and harsh." The choicest human relations are at best unstable on this transitory stage, where we meet and part as "ships that pass in the night."

Institutions become ossified and fail to respond to our needs. Civilizations are turned to ashes in the senseless conflicts of men. The objects of our earthly hopes and aspirations are made of fragile stuff. In the midst of the changes and chances of this mortal life we long for a stable object of loyalty. When our faith meets with shipwreck in our human temporal world, we pray in our distress, "O Thou, who changest not, abide with me." We seek for one who is the same yesterday, today, and forever, with whom is neither variableness nor shadow of turning. Again, we supplement the fickle weather of an actual world with an ideal world of values. And if we find ourselves mistaken about eternal truths and if sacred time-honored institutions prove to be old bottles which cannot hold the new wine of progress, we attach our faith amid the wreckage of time to the spirit of truth which abides, to a kingdom not of this world. We feel that in some way there must be an eternal and intrinsic world of values which can give significance and worth to the fleeting values of our passing lives — an eternal ideal

of good for which we can strive and in which we can put our
trust though all else crumbles.

In the world in which the soul finds itself there seems to be
a constant disharmony between what we feel ought to be, the
soul's dream of right and beauty, and the world as it actually
is. There is much ugliness, much that is wrong within and without. The evil forces often seem to triumph. "The wicked
flourish like a green bay tree." Lying and deceit seem for the
time being more successful than truth and right-doing. The
forces of this world mock us and say "Where is now thy God?"
Life, from the narrow perspective that we see, spells failure
at best. It has been said that every animal life is a tragedy. How
much truer that is of human life. Our best purposes are frus-
trated. How insignificant the accomplishment of the greatest
life compared with the task that it has set itself. It often seems
the labor of Sisyphus rolling a stone that ever rolls back, the
vain longing of Tantalus for the water that ever recedes.
"Vanity of vanities" seems written over the whole of man's
futile efforts. And the most tragic failure of all is not to
realize the failure, but to live in illusory content.

In this world of maladjustment and evil the soul raises its
protest. The universe cannot be so blind, so disregardful of our
ideals, as it seems. At least we may retain faith in our own
dignity and may grit our teeth and redouble our efforts at the
oar, with a dumb willingness to risk and with the venturesomeness of Tennyson's Ulysses:

> . . Strong in will
> To strive, to seek, to find and not to yield.
> . . . For my purpose holds
> To sail beyond the sunset and the paths
> Of all the western stars, until I die.
> It may be that the gulfs will wash us down;
> It may be we shall touch the Happy Isles.
> . . . But something ere the end,
> Some work of noble note may yet be done.

Is there in this human world no spring of budding hope, no summer of fruition to follow "the winter of our discontent?" Shall we drink the cup of bitterness alone? Shall we bear the whole burden of life? Shall there be child labor, white slavery, and war, and God not care? Is not this feeling of disharmony begotten of the universe that brought us forth? And shall it be indifferent to our protest and efforts? The understanding of life's problem in the large is beyond us. But faith springs up afresh in the human heart that life has meaning. We cannot say with nineteenth century romanticism:

> God's in his heaven,
> All's right with the world.

There is terrible tragedy in the world because of man's blindness. But we must remember that great historic movements require time. There is a force, we believe, greater than ourselves, which works for righteousness and which, with our cooperation, shapes our human destiny, long though the task may be. Though there is much that is bad in us, the good shall somehow triumph. A remnant shall survive. The loyal Servant of Jehovah shall not labor and suffer in vain. Perhaps in the very struggle, born of the faith in the right, lies the victory. At least we are not utterly forsaken in our endeavors. Though the journey be hard, the goal is worth the struggle.

In some vision of beauty the ugliness shall disappear. In some symphony of life the discord shall be unified. If we do not grow weary of well-doing the right shall finally triumph. Thus the soul builds out an ideal world of right and beauty to compensate for this marred and inharmonious world of ours.

But what about the individual soul and its destiny? Is the promise only to the race in its endless striving, or perhaps to the endless aeons of the cosmic universe? Shall we fall by the way that others may rise on our dead selves to a nobler destiny? Is our little troubled consciousness to be extinguished like a

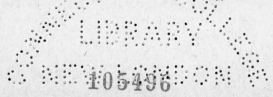

candle in the night? How much there is within us which fails of expression in this little life! How much that is suppressed or dormant because a disordered environment fails to call it forth from its living tomb! How many a life is blasted in the midst of its promise, "as oft a rough wind sheds the unripe promise of a field flower." Is this life of ours, so pregnant with unfulfilled hopes and yearnings, to be utterly barren of fulfilment? Is love's dream to prove a hollow mockery, all because of blind chance?

Again, the human heart raises its protest, in the ringing words of Browning:

> God! Thou art mind. Unto the master mind
> Mind should be precious. Spare my mind alone.
>
> . . . .
>
> Yet God is good.

And though death seems to triumph and the dear lips are still and the hand is cold, though earth closes over the fair form and the green grass heals the scar of its resting-place, love will not have it that it is the end; but like a sweet angel proclaims over the grave: "He is not here, but is risen." What moulders here "is but his shadow. His substance is not here." The universe shall not permit that which has significance and worth to perish.

There is an instinct within us which insists that this life is but a moment, a fragment, of an unseen larger life in which it has its true setting. Much there is, no doubt, that is of earth, earthy in what this instinct craves, many vain hopes and desires which echo the carnal disappointment of this world. Our insight is frail at best, and our love does not always understand itself. But the human mind insists that somehow the world of death shall be supplemented by a world of immortality, that what an eternal love finds unique and valuable shall not perish from the universe.

Religion and the Proportion of Values

Another function of religion is to give us the right perspective of life, to establish the proper proportion of values. The instincts that grovel at the bottom of our nature are getting far more than their share of our interest. We are thinking far too much of our eating and drinking, of our sense gratifications. For these we are altogether too ready to barter away our spiritual heritage. We think far too little of our common good and too much of our individual comfort. We need a Wordsworth to awaken us from our indifference.

> The world is too much with us. Late and soon,
> Getting and spending, we lay waste our powers:
> Little we see in nature that is ours;
> We have given our hearts away, a sordid boon!
> This sea that bares her bosom to the moon;
> The winds that will be howling at all hours,
> And are upgathered now like sleeping flowers:
> For this, for everything, we are out of tune;
> It moves us not — Great God! I'd rather be
> A pagan suckled in a creed outworn;
> So might I standing on this pleasant lea,
> Have glimpses that would make me less forlorn;
> Have sight of Proteus rising from the sea;
> Or hear old Triton blow his wreathed horn.

It is the function of religion to teach us to set first things first. "Seek ye first the kingdom of God and his righteousness, and all these shall be added unto you." In order to correct our distorted perspective of values it may indeed be necessary to overemphasize, to overcorrect. Were there danger of overemphasizing the spiritual, we might have to exhort with Browning:

> Let us not always say,
> "Spite of this flesh today
> I strove, made head, gained ground upon the whole!"

As the bird wings and sings,
Let us cry, "All good things
Are ours, nor soul helps flesh
More now, than flesh helps soul!"

Flesh does have its rightful claims. We cannot ignore the primitive instincts without committing suicide. But in most of us flesh is too strongly fortified to need further defense. We must ceaselessly batter down its self-contented immurement by preaching the kingdom of the good of the whole, of the future generations as well as the present. We must relearn again and again the lesson of renunciation, "lest we forget, lest we forget." Perhaps in this way the pendulum of life may swing nearer to the golden mean. We may be sure that, if we once learn to put first things first, other things will fall into their proper order. To build our civilization on material efficiency alone and neglect the poetry, the farther ideal reaches of life, is to brutalize man, is to lose the proper control of the primitive within us and to invite just such a crisis as that which is visiting Europe today, where material and spiritual values are alike in danger of being buried in the general chaos. We must learn sanity of perspective. And that we can do only by seeing things, as Spinoza would say, *sub specie aeternitatis,* by learning to think in terms of the whole of life. Only the religious devotion to a common ideal can enforce this lesson upon a short-sighted, self-seeking race, be its blindness individual or national. Of the two, national selfishness has shown itself to be the more dangerous.

It is true that conventional religion has often joined in conspiracy with men's passions, reinforcing their blindness by somnolent acquiescence or misdirected devotion, following the flag of man's selfish lust for power. But for true religion no ideal short of humanity can suffice. Its cause must be the common good of man. Its loyalty is limited by no national or race boundaries. For there can be no true loyalty to a nation which is not at the same time loyalty to humanity. We can worship no national god. Spiritually and materially our destiny is interlinked. And sectional hate and strife must prove suicidal to true human realization. We must learn to think in terms of the whole. Our rivalry must be to realize the best. Our conquest must be by superior and more beneficent ideals. There is beauty, it is true, in the devoted loyalty of the youth of many lands in the tragedy through which the world is passing. The pity is that "someone has blundered," that millions through the blindness of their leaders and a false philosophy are sacrificed for an unworthy cause. And no cause can be worthy except the melioration of our human lot, the improvement and happiness of humanity.

This loyalty to a human cause must mean devotion to the future race as well as to the present. What about man a million years from now? In looking backward we can see that the faltering steps and sacrifice of man's upward march are more significant for us than they could have been for man then and there. It is by his struggles and failures that our achievements have been made possible. We are part of a great march of life. Our efforts, too, are steps in the upward climb of man. Shall we be unmindful of the promise of the race? Shall we by our selfishness cut short the journey to the higher goal? Shall humanity fail in its destiny because of our lack of faith? We must build, even as the bee builds, for generations which we cannot see, guided by an instinctive faith which, wiser than it knows, constructs the destiny of a nobler future — a faith in the promise of a redeemed and happy humanity. Thus religion furnishes us a new center of insight and energy which gives us both a true perspective of values and fresh inspiration for their realization. We shall hate, not each other, but whatever degrades and debases us. We shall love and cherish whatever is eternally human.

Religion and the Initiation into Social Values

Religion from time immemorial has had for its function to initiate the individual into the solemn obligations of our social life. It has made the vital bonds of our common life sacred and momentous, and by this primary impression, and the faith back of it, has tended to make them stable. It has made every important human bond a bond with the divine as well. It lies about us like heaven in our infancy, and by its constructive faith makes us members of the spiritual community. With solemn vows it initiates us into the new consciousness of youth and idealizes its pressing instincts into activities for beauty, right, and truth. It hallows love's dream and makes it a marriage of true souls. When we stumble and fall under the burden of the day it takes us by the hand and reinstates us into the kingdom of usefulness and love. At the portal of every great opportunity it sanctifies the task and gives us renewed courage. It consecrates our earthly bonds of friendship and calls us to friendship with God. It stays with us through the livelong day and widens our sympathies for a larger life with men. It blesses our gray hairs and transforms the lines of age into the expressions of a benevolent soul. When the shadows lengthen and eventide comes it prepares us for the final mysteries and "gives to His beloved sleep;" and when life's fitful fever is over it proclaims over our ashes the gospel of eternal hope.

Religion thus makes sacramental and sacred our vital human bonds. Can human institutions stand without it? Without its halo of divinity will human obligations prove inviting and enduring? Will the family and other institutions crumble under the weight of human selfishness? In the new stresses and strains of life we need more than ever the solemn consecration of the religious consciousness — its emphasis that true human obligations are also divine obligations; that initiation into human life at every step must also, in order to insure real success and happiness, be an initiation into the Kingdom of Heaven; that God calls us to devotion to the great common tasks of life.

Religion and the Conservation of Values

Religion emphasizes loyalty to the spiritual heritage of the past. It is the great conservative agency, the balance wheel of society. It insists upon the importance of holding fast to that which we have attained. Civilization is but of yesterday. There is the constant danger of sliding back to the level of the savage and the brute. Witness today the spectacle of some of the most cultured nations disregarding the restraints of civilization and demolishing, in the blindness of hate, not only all the material monuments of civilization, but all those human bonds which we have regarded as sacred. What shall it profit us that by means of science we have, as never before, become masters of nature's forces on land, in the air, and under the sea, if we in our blindness use these forces to blow each other out of existence? Of what avail is it that we create beautiful cathedrals and masterful art if in our animal fury we reduce the work of centuries to ashes? Why build institutions of learning and bring out splendid youth if we are going to use them as "cannon fodder?" Of what avail is our great industry, with its magnificent machinery, if we become slaves of our own tools and reduce human beings to a sordid and unhappy existence? Of what use are all our culture and wealth if we are going to be the prey of our primitive and selfish impulses? Of what use is thought itself, the noblest of human endowments, if it loses its fundamental motive for constructiveness, turns upon itself, and eats out its own heart? Is this great civilization, which it has taken a million years to launch, to founder on the rocks of our selfish blindness? We need a wholesome reverence for what the race has established in the way of principles of right if civilization is not going to suffer shipwreck. Nothing but a profound religious sense of the sacredness of the obligations of man to man can hope to hold against the fierce instincts of envy and hate in our primitive nature. It still holds true as of old: "Except the Lord build the house, they labor in vain that build it." Religion, with its consciousness of the guardianship of God over what the race has so dearly won, is the essential cement in holding our social structure together.

Today more than ever we need restraint and thoughtfulness in the complex social readjustments of which we are a part. New social forces have been liberated. New problems must be met. In the clashing of the interests of individuals, classes, and nations how shall we maintain our poise until new solutions have been arrived at? In our restless desire for change we must not forget the lessons of human experience. Mere uncontrolled change is anarchy, a ship without balast, an engine without brakes running downhill toward a bridgeless chasm. We cannot afford to throw away the controls of the past in steering toward the new dangers of the future. It is true that religion has too often been interpreted as the maintenance of vested privilege, as the bulwark of the inequalities of man, as the sanction for things as they are as against the forward-looking instinct of justice. But true religious loyalty is not slavery to the past. It is the due regard for human claims. It is the maintenance of peace and order, of mutual regard and forbearance, while our conflicting interests are being adjusted into a common life. Religion must be, above all, loyalty to an ideal social order. But this can only be realized as a fulfilment of the past, not in breaking away from the past.

The meaning of the religious sanctions must indeed vary with man's social development. Our old ideas of heaven and hell were taken over from a savage imagination and are no longer real to us. Our old idea of God was reminiscent of an antiquated social order. But some faith there must be in justice

working through the laws of the universe. "The soul that sinneth it shall die." As of old, so always, God is the guardian of
our common life. The bond that binds us together is not a
mere concern of man, but a sacramental bond, a partnership
with God. In the absence of such a supernatural sanction,
bridling man's individual and collective selfishness, it is hard
to see how human institutions can hold together. Religion takes
its stand for the momentous values of society. It restrains our
impatience, our fickle, momentary impulses, in order that our
common life may prosper. True, it has often been confused in
its insight. It has sometimes emphasized form rather than
substance, etiquette rather than morality. It has often in its
institutional capacity been blind to new truth. It has crucified
the prophets that were sent while building tombs to the
prophets that had been. But its instinct of social preservation
has ever been sound. It has not willingly let go the old values
until the new have been tried out. It has held the line against
the forces that would press us back to the chaos whence we
came, while through its consecrated prophets it has tried to
furnish a workable plan for the future.

Religion as Creative Interpretation

It is a mistake to regard the conservative function as the only
function of religion. Religion manifests its deepest nature as
a creative factor in human life. Not in the church quiescent
with its somnolent phrases and its backward look, but in the
church militant with its zeal for righteousness, with its forward
look, courses the life blood of religion. Religion needs not
merely its priests with their guardianship of the past, but even
more its prophets creating the future. For religion is not fundamentally a set of institutions and ceremonies, but a life, and
the life of religion is a moving onward to a larger expression,
to higher and nobler embodiments.

Not that we should despise the achievements of the past, or that we should fail to honor the heroic dead. But loyalty to the great leaders of the past means that we carry their work onward to further completion. We cannot win the goal which the past strove and sacrificed to attain by standing still. We can be true to the spirit of the past only by continued growth, not by atrophy. It is the function of religion ever to use the heritage of the past in living exchange, not to bury it. The present must ever be the fulfilment of the law and the prophets, not their graveyard. We are truest to the past vision when we look forward, not when we look backward. We must share with the great souls of the past the infinite promise of the future.

The prophet is a man who lives in presence of reality. He walks in the light as God gives him to see the light. His countenance like that of Moses shines with the presence of God. He uses past attainments as stepping stones while he mounts

> "Upon the great world's altar stairs
> That slope thro' darkness up to God" —

not faltering or chafing, but firm in the larger hope. He is, in the words of Carlyle, "a messenger, sent from the Infinite Unknown with tidings to us. We may call him Poet, Prophet, God; — in one way or another, we all feel that the words he utters are as no other man's words. Direct from the Inner Fact of things; — he lives, and has to live, in daily communion with that. Hearsays cannot hide it from him. . . . It is from the heart of the world that he comes; he is portion of the primal reality of things. . . . Fearful and wonderful, real as Life, real as Death, is this Universe to him. Though all men should forget its truth and walk in a vain show, he cannot. At all moments the Flame-image glares in upon him; undeniable, there, there!"

He does not cry peace, peace, when there is no peace. His is the battle cry of justice and the love for a greater humanity. His mission is not to administer a soporific to a guilty conscience; his is a call to repentance. He furnishes the incentive, yea the goad, to a new life; he awakes us to our imperfection and the reality of the ideal. He gives us of his own — his own deep experience of man and God. He does not deal with life second-hand. He speaks with the authority of firsthand insight. He is the living torch of the ages, its incarnate wisdom. "Thus saith the Lord."

He does not speak gibberish, as sometimes supposed, but interprets the real life of his age and his people. He deals with the real present and tries to reconstruct the past to meet present needs. In thus doing he builds unconsciously for the future. Because he is in the succession of the spiritual wisdom of the ages, he is wiser than he knows. His is not a wisdom, "cut from love and faith," but the awakening soul of the ages pressing forward to its destiny. He represents the vanguard of civilization. He is the true pioneer of humanity. Whether he uses words or tones or marble as his symbols, he wins new soul, creates new ideals for the race — ideals of cooperation and achievement. Because he is wiser than his age, he is always misunderstood and usually persecuted by the vested interests of the past. But he is the leaven of a nobler order which is bound to win in the end, because it makes possible wiser and more beneficent human cooperation. He is the living harbinger of the kingdom of heaven. He is the searchlight which God casts into the future. He is the life of religion.

Religion as Communion with God

The final and all-inclusive function of religion is communion with God. It converts what would otherwise be an abstract ideal into a consciousness of real Presence. It attunes our souls into living harmony with the divine. This presence takes different forms in our life in accordance with our experience and temperament. It may be the stern call to duty, the sublimity of the moral law in our soul, more awesome than the starry heavens above. It may be the infinite friendliness of a life that envelops us even as the atmosphere. It may be a vision into the deeper meaning of life with its infinite reaches. But always it means the sense of companionship and cooperation with God. Always it pervades life like some sweet melody and melts its discord into harmony. Like new blood, it flows into the veins of our life and gives us strength. Always it expands our better self and makes it dominate the conflicting impulses of our nature. Always it means charity, forgiveness, and helpfulness to all our humankind. Always it means friendship with man and God. It is a sixth sense of the soul, opening up to it the enveloping reality of the ideal beauty and goodness.

Today more than ever, in the stress and strain of modern society, we need the transforming consciousness of that eternal Presence, working for redemption from our selfishness and isolation, for wholeness in our conception of life, for sacrificing love in the realization of the purpose of the race. This consciousness of the living presence of the spirit of God in humanity, reinforcing its ideals, leading in its upward struggle, healing the wounds of fraternal strife, is the only force strong enough to keep humanity from disintegrating and sufficient to mold its divergent interests into loyalty to a comprehensive cause. In the sign of the cross alone, the symbol of devoted sacrifice for the whole, can we conquer. The Kingdom of God is the only salt of the earth which can keep life from losing its savor, the only light which can guide humanity to a common goal.

Is this ideal world of our striving an illusory oasis in the desert? Is this creative building out of life but a tissue of fairy tales, woven by our will to believe? Is this sense of peace, in companionship with the divine, but a lullaby by which we

wretched mortals soothe ourselves to sleep? Shall we waken
with a shock to the naked reality of matter in motion, a world
void of ideals and meaning? So materialism preaches with
supreme confidence in many quarters and in many insidious
forms. For it the satisfaction of our animal lusts is the final
reality of life; the overweening instinct for power is the final
arbiter of destiny. Of this philosophy of life we are now
eating the bitter fruits. I prefer to believe with the noble
idealists of all time that our ideal yearnings, crude though
they are in content, are homing instincts, orienting us to our
Father's house; that in them somehow the universe which
brought us forth gives us its intimations of our place and goal.
With Wordsworth, I thank God, not so much for the "delight
and liberty" attained,

> But for those obstinate questionings
> Of sense and outward things,
> Fallings from us, vanishings;
> Blank misgivings of a creature
> Moving about in worlds not realized,
> High instincts before which our mortal nature
> Did tremble like a guilty thing surprised,
>
> . . . .
>
> Which, be they what they may,
> Are yet the fountain light of all our day,
> Are yet a master light of all our seeing:
> Uphold us, cherish, and have power to make
> Our noisy years seem moments in the being
> Of the eternal silence.

The world of sense, of solid mechanism, is but an island
floating in the larger world of spiritual forces and deriving its
direction and significance from it. We are not duped when we
believe that the dice of the universe are loaded for right and
reason. It is only so that we can have sanity and understanding.
Else the world were a mad dance of chance. Only so can the
universe furnish us with a vocation suitable to the nature it

has given us. Else were life a grim joke. Only so can we realize a happy humanity.

> Hence in a season of calm weather
> Though inland far we be,
> Our souls have sight of that immortal sea
> Which brought us hither,
> Can in a moment travel thither,
> And see the children sport upon the shore
> And hear the mighty waters rolling evermore.

PART ONE

THE CONSCIOUSNESS OF THE DIVINE

CHAPTER TWO

THE SENSE OF PRESENCE AND
INTELLECTUAL ABSTRACTION

Man, since first he emerged in the dim past, has lived in the presence of the supernatural. Even the men of the Old Stone Age believed in something more than the apparent world. The burial customs of the Neanderthal man show that he believed in life after death. And the paintings of the Cromagnon man bear evidence that he used magic, and magic implies a belief in supernatural powers. As man reacts instinctively to a world of things and selves, so he reacts instinctively to the spiritual world about him. In some way, however crude, he has tried to establish relations with the divine about him and within him. Early religion was concrete and intuitive. Man felt the presence of supernatural powers everywhere and endeavored in his own way to appease their anger and to win their favor. This sense of a mysterious presence was not, to primitive man, a mere social symbol but a living reality, though it got its content then as always from human relations and in turn reacted upon these to make them stable and meaningful. There was a spirit in the tree, in the river, in the high places, in the cloud and in the wind, but it was always a particular presence with a particular character of friendliness or unfriendliness, always potent to work good or ill. Such a simple religion could not help evoking the scorn of the shallow rationalism of Pope:

"Lo, the poor Indian! whose untutored mind
Sees God in clouds, or hears him in the wind.
His soul proud science never taught to stray
Far as the solar walk or milky way."

Gods were local beings. They lived in definite places. And
however men might wander, they were certain that the god
whose help they might need would abide constantly in the place
where he was discovered. He belongs to the soil. And so it was
that the primitive patriarch, fallen asleep under the desert sky
and awaking out of his dream, in which he had seen the
heavens open and angels ascending and descending, felt:
"Surely, the Lord is in this place and I knew it not." And he
called the place, Bethel, the house of God, and built there an
altar and made a vow to return and sacrifice if the Lord pros-
pered him. At a later stage of religious development, Moses
refused to leave Mount Sinai, the home of the lightning God
Jehovah, until he felt assured that Jehovah could somehow send
his presence: "And He said, My presence shall go with thee
and I will give thee rest." "And he said unto him, if thy
presence go not with me, carry us not hence." It was such a
feeling for the soil that led Naaman, the Syrian, to request
the favor of taking some of the soil of Israel with him to his
native city in order that he might worship his new-found God
there.

There is something beautifully simple and real about this
early religion. It lacks, to be sure, in abstract theory and in
universality of perspective. Man had not yet arrived at the
consciousness which would enable him to

"See the genius of the whole
Ascendant in the private souls."

The divine presence was limited not only to local shrines but
to local needs. Yet, at least, he felt the reality of the divine
presence in the particular situations of life. He had not substituted words for reality. We are not far removed from primitive

man in our instinctive needs. We, too, are of the soil and our
emotional roots cling to localities and symbols which experience has hallowed to us, because we have sensed the presence
of the divine in some particular life setting. Every sincere soul
has its Bethel, its place of supreme loyalty. You may seek the
whole world over, but earth never touches heaven anywhere
as it does where the soul first discovers the profounder meaning
of life. There is God's house. Nor is it true that nature and
God are so sharply separated as our modern abstractions have
made them appear. There is more to the cloud and the wind
as appreciated by the soul of the poet than physical science
can ever compress within its formulae. There is, somehow, in
the moment of genuine appreciation and devotion, a creative
synthesis in which the divine genius of the universe enters as an
active agent. And the concrete setting is part of this synthesis
and makes it unique. Modern science says that nature is a collection of interacting elements and that the laws of nature are
only statistical averages; but primitive intuition is right, that
really to understand nature, in its creative variety and unity,
you must recognize the divine factor in nature. We need more
than science. We need also poetry and religion if we are to
discover the soul of things, the creative genius in nature.

This sense of the unity of mind with the creative soul in
nature makes communion a reality instead of mere words. How
beautiful it is to feel with the ancient Greeks the divine
presence in the woods! What could be more exquisite and sincere than the prayer which Plato puts in the mouth of Socrates
at the end of the *Phaedrus?* "Beloved Pan and all ye other Gods
who haunt this place, give me beauty in the inward soul and
may the outward and the inward man be at one. May I reckon
the wise to be the wealthy and may I have such a quantity of
gold as only the temperate can carry. Anything more, no I think
that is enough for me." In a mystical mood, we may feel with
Richard Realf:

"All shapes and sounds have something which is not
Of them: a spirit broods amid the grass;
Vague outlines of the Everlasting Thought
Lie in the melting shadows as they pass;
The touch of an Eternal Presence thrills
The fringes of the sunsets and the hills."

Primitive man, while unable thus to express himself in language, felt the divine presence in "the sunsets and the hills," drawing him mysteriously to the high places where he built his shrines. It was not with him as with the sophisticated modern pantheist an identification of God and nature, but the sensing of something in nature beyond the seen, which speaks somehow directly to the creative soul of man and speaks a different language, becomes a different presence with different conditions. The emphasis in the primitive soul is on the presences, the intimate, various first-hand continuities of the soul with the unseen. The idea of *the* Presence as one and invariable came as the result of man's social evolution and abstract thought.

The victorious march of evolution from local presences and local shrines to the monotheistic conception of the divine as one essence, present everywhere and always, is counted one of the greatest achievements of man. Yet civilization is bought with a price. There are losses as well as compensations in that greater unification of life and thought which marks the intellectual progress of the race. And nowhere is this more clearly seen than in the developing of the idea of God. The tendency has been to lose the sense of the intimate presence of the divine, vitally affecting every function of everyday life, and to substitute, for the personal relation which simpler souls have felt, an abstract God who is aloof from our individual concerns and with whom our relations are necessarily impersonal. We have intellectualized the spiritual relation instead of making it first of all feeling and conduct. It is a significant parallelism that transcendental monotheism and mechanism have developed together, for both are the products of the abstract intellect, rather than the reaction of our whole personal life. Nor can we dismiss the matter by saying that the abstract conceptions work better, for what we call civilization is only of yesterday, and the utter failure of the religion of some highly cultured peoples today to offer any restraint to their primitive, even if intellectualized, instincts is a serious challenge to our easy optimism as regards progress. Cain may boast of the superiority of his tools and organization, yet the blood of the simpler more sincere souls which he supplants cries to heaven. One thing is certain: the earlier more intimate type of religion was potent to restrain men's impulses and our modern abstract religion does not seem to be able to do so.

Yet we cannot return to the past. Life is always in evolution. There are two reasons for the rapid changes which a religion like that of the ancient Hebrews underwent. One was the development of language. It was a sound instinct of the primitive heart when it tried to taboo any name for the divine. For a name soon brings radical changes in the development of an idea. The symbol inevitably tends to take the place of the reality. Yet language is indispensable to social development. Where people mean the same kind of thing and where they are bound together by common interest and common activities, there must be some way of identifying the common bond and the sacred feelings which are associated with it. "I am that I am," which was meant as a taboo of a name, itself becomes a name. After man gave a name to what he felt to be divine, he proceeded to personify it, to create it in his own likeness, to interpret it in terms of his own human relations — shepherd, patriarch, judge, king, and last of all the great companion and friend. Man must necessarily appreciate God through human relations. He cannot be wiser than his experience. But we must not forget that all such ways of characterizing the divine are inadequate. While God does reveal himself in finite human relations, He is always infinitely more; and the more can come to us only with the deeper cultivation of the soul. At best our experience is partial and inadequate. At best our intellect sees darkly through the medium of its tradition, and our feelings may be deeper than our abstract thoughts. The latter tend to be largely symbols of a reality of which the soul has somehow an intimation and which it strives in vain to express.

There was, in the second place, a social and political reason for the rapid change in the Hebrew idea of God. The tribal organization broke down in Israel's struggle for survival against better organized neighbors. For the creating of a national bond, it was necessary to have a common flag or symbol of loyalty; and Jehovah, the God of the Hebrews in the desert, free from local associations, provided such a rallying point. At first there was no conscious conflict between a national God and local gods. The local shrines were still objects of reverence in the days of Saul and David; and Solomon, too, when he wished guidance for his career, went to one of the celebrated high places where God came to him in a dream and granted him the boon of wisdom. Nor, even after the building of the national temple, do Solomon and his successors seem to have abandoned the worship at local shrines.

It was left for the great prophets of Israel to carry on the campaign against the high places. There were two reasons for their relentless zeal against these. One was the recognition that only in a strong national unity could there be any hope for Israel against its powerful neighbors. The high places stood for localism and tribalism. The temple in Jerusalem with its Jehovah worship stood for nationalism. The extermination of the high places meant, therefore, in the minds of the prophets, loyalty to the national cause. Only through the consciousness of such national unity could Israel realize its vocation as a chosen people. Jerusalem was the apple of Jehovah and in his safe keeping. There, and only there, with the ark and the sacred symbols, was Jehovah's presence to be sought. "The Lord is in his holy temple, let all the earth keep silence before Him." It was still a local presence. Jehovah was still the God of the soil, but he stood for relations more inclusive than those of the old tribal shrines. The people, however, were naturally reluctant to give up their intimate local associations for the more remote presence in Jerusalem, and the efforts of the prophets met with only sporadic success before the Exile. The other reason for the zeal of the prophets against the local cults was a moral one. The local cults represented more primitive customs, a lower stage of morality, than that which the prophets were attempting to introduce into the national conception of Jehovah. Hence the local loyalties were regarded not merely as infidelity to the national cause but as the prostitution of a more advanced moral consciousness of which Jehovah had become the symbol.

The Exile was a severe shock to the religious foundations of Judaism. The lantern of Jehovah was destroyed, contrary to the theory of the prophets before the Exile. Jehovah, who had been thought of as living in Jerusalem and as being bound up exclusively with the Hebrew nation and the Hebrew soil, was expatriated. How indeed could the children of Israel be expected to "sing the songs of Zion in a strange land?" But an unknown prophet, whom we call "the Second Isaiah," the Hebrews' greatest poet, came to the rescue of the bankrupt religion of Israel with a new interpretation. It was not Israel as a nation which was Jehovah's supreme care, but the loyal portion of Israel, the faithful remnant, the suffering servant of Jehovah. This remnant was still in Jehovah's keeping. Jehovah's cause would still triumph. This new faith in Jehovah was supported by a more transcendent conception of his presence in the cosmos. He is not dependent upon Jerusalem for his abode nor upon the might of the Hebrew people. "It is he that sitteth upon the circle of the earth and the inhabitants thereof are as grasshoppers; that stretcheth out the heavens as a curtain, and spreadeth them out as a tent to dwell in." He marshals the hosts of heaven by name; to him nations are as a drop in the bucket; he can use them, friendly or hostile, in the realization of his cosmic purposes. A lofty conception indeed as compared to the images made by men's hands. In this new conception of Jehovah are vested all the attributes of justice, mercy, might and wisdom which mark the climax of Hebrew monotheism.

But lofty as this conception was, it was abstract and seemed to remove God from human relations. It could not have kept alive the faith of the Hebrews without the more concrete appeal —Ezekiel's vision of the new temple, with its cult and sense of local presence. In due time, Israel was permitted by a foreign servant of Jehovah to rebuild its temple and to re-establish its national worship in Jerusalem. The generation which returned from Babylon knew nothing of local associations; and the calamity which the prophets had attributed to worship at local shrines ensured the centralized religion of Israel. With the centralization developed the abstractness of the idea of God. He became like unto a man who had gone into a far country. There was indeed loyalty to the national worship, and at times sublime sacrifice for it; but the tendency of the new cult was to substitute an elaborate ritualism and technical ceremonialism for a presence which reveals itself directly in sincere and loyal human relations. And with the fading away of the consciousness of the real presence, materialism and scepticism exhorted men to enjoy the pleasure of the moment as the gift of God rather than trouble themselves with "some after reckoning ta'en on trust." This attitude found its expression in the author of *Ecclesiastes*, the Omar Khayyam of the Hebrews. Even in devout circles, a cold Pharisaism was the institutional counterpart of a transcendent God. Religion became a technical affair and remote from personal relations.

The more devout souls sought to satisfy their craving for a

personal God, present and effective in human affairs, in apocalyptic mysticism — the dream of a God who was soon to come
in splendor and make his kingdom prevail over the hostile
powers of the world. And this passionate hope for a return of
God to a world which had been allowed to run itself and had
run amuck, or even had become the ally of evil powers, kept
alive their faith in times of great tribulation. However fantastic
may be the symbolism of the apocalyptic period, it was the
manifestation of a new idealism in a sordid and decadent
world. And it appealed to the human heart. It made possible
the victory of a new religion. For Christianity could hardly have
won the world except for the apocalyptic feature — the promise
of the return of God and the near and dramatic triumph of
good over evil. Jesus became identified with the hero of the
apocalyptic drama — the son of man who should return in his
glory and all his angels with him.

CHAPTER THREE

CHRISTIANITY AND THE NEW SENSE
OF PRESENCE

With Jesus of Nazareth there comes a new consciousness of God's presence. The immortal discovery of Jesus is that the kingdom of heaven is within us. No need of journeying long distances to find God. His sanctuary may be, and must be, if we are to find Him, in our inmost soul. It is true that Jesus is loyal to the national religion. The temple in Jerusalem is still for him his Father's house. Thither his soul yearns to keep holy-day with his people, and not even the danger of death could keep him away. The purging of the national temple, so as to make it indeed a house of prayer, no doubt hastened the end of his career. Jesus does not despise the outward and social setting. But there is not only one Jerusalem where God may be found. Each soul has its own Jerusalem. The holy of holies is in men's hearts when they are in tune with the divine. This does not mean that God reveals himself only in solitude, though Jesus himself finds it necessary to withdraw at times into the silence of his soul. The kingdom of heaven is a social kingdom, a kingdom of helpfulness, of friendship. He promises a peculiar grace where two or three are gathered together for a holy purpose. His last public act was a sacrament which was to become the communion of the faithful, bound together by his death. Nor was he indifferent to nature. He found the divine inspiration peculiarly in the high places as instanced by the Sermon on the Mount, the Mount of Transfiguration and the Mount of Olives, though he found God in the desert, too, and on the stormy waters. Nature to him was not mean and degraded but instinct with the presence of God. He saw God's providence in the lilies of the field and in the fate of the humble sparrow.

The presence of God was with Jesus a simple concrete intuition, which he felt and which he lived in human relations, not an abstract philosophy. It is a presence which is near and possible to every man, which manifests itself indeed in all his better moments. It is not the monopoly of the learned. Indeed the sophisticated of this world are particularly blind. It requires merely the willing, pure, sincere, and earnest heart to see God. The kingdom of heaven is at hand. Godward there is the open door, though manward the door is often closed by our selfishness and prejudice. This religion of Jesus is not a vague pantheism. Everything is not divine, there is much to overcome. We must make violence upon the kingdom of heaven. We can only conquer by prayer and fasting. Yet it is a joyous life, this life in God. And the presence of God is a democratic presence, ever ready to transform the lowliest and even outcast lives — publicans and sinners, the penitent thief on the cross. It is closed only to the hypocrite, the insincere of heart. How simple, sweet, delicate, tender, yet stern to combat evil is this life of Jesus in the presence of God — claiming nothing for himself except service and sacrifice. No wonder he draws the world to himself and to the presence in which he lives. The idealistic revival of the Galilean unites the intimacy of a primitive intuition with a monotheistic perspective.

The faith in the incarnation of God in Jesus rests upon the recognition of Jesus as the incarnation of divine goodness. He liberated, shed, created goodness in all his relations with men, and continues to do so. He increases the maximum of goodness wherever his influence is felt; and therefore we feel that he is divine. Our faith does not rest upon the stories of his miraculous conception nor upon the miracles reported to have been performed by Him. Such stories abound in the biographies of the great religious leaders of the past in various religions, but we do not, therefore, accept them. Creeds, theories, do not make Jesus or anyone else divine. They merely register in a clumsy and transient fashion our perennial faith in his goodness. The intuition of the continuity of God with man in Jesus of Nazareth is the basic fact of Christianity. Once the presence of God is brought back from the high heavens of human abstraction, a new force for goodness is liberated, which is bound to spread until it affects our entire attitude to man and the universe.

It was this intuition of the real presence of God in human life that the age of theory and creed-making tried to express. The important thing for us is to distinguish and to save the intuition from the man-made theories to explain the fact. The fact must indeed be assimilated into the matrix of beliefs which are vital at the time. Early Christianity had its own background and setting; it tried to translate the life of Jesus into its own thought-world. There is the ideal expressed by the second Isaiah, of the suffering and victorious Servant of Jehovah who by his good tidings and his vicarious sacrifice comes to heal a broken world. This is the ideal that Jesus himself preaches to his hearers as realized before their eyes. There is also the persistence of the messianic hope of the apocalyptic period. This hope is now transformed into the belief of the early return of Jesus in power and glory, and greatly heartened the early Christians in days of persecution. Very early, too, comes the interpretation of the life of Jesus in terms of the priestly tradition of the Jewish church, as we can see in the *Epistle to the Hebrews*. In this interpretation, Jesus plays the part at once of high priest and of vicarious offering, atoning once for all by his supreme sacrifice for the sins of the world. This ideal became an important element in the tradition of Christianity. Finally, there is the attempt to assimilate the intuition of Jesus into a certain philosophy of the day, unknown to the Synoptic Gospels. The opening of the Fourth Gospel is a paraphrase of the philosophy of Philo, the Jew, which is here given a Christian application. Jesus is identified with "the Word," the *Logos,* the divine wisdom, which was with God in the beginning, through which the world was made and which mediates between a transcendent God and the world. This "Word," according to the Fourth Gospel, became flesh in Jesus of Nazareth, the glory of the only begotten, full of grace and truth.

The stage is now set for the centuries of creed making. When Jesus had been identified with "the Word," there arose first the question: What is the relation of the incarnate Word to God? Is he a created being, and, therefore, lower in rank than God, as Arius preached at the beginning of the fourth century, or is he really continuous with God, "begotten of the Father before all worlds, God of God, light of light, very God of very God, begotten not made, being of one essence with the Father, and was made man," as expressed in the Nicene creed in 325 A.D.? It is a long and intricate story, in which not a little sordid politics of the will-to-power, of persecution and counterpersecution, is mixed in. But the Christian community, in the end, holds on to the intuition of the real presence of God in Jesus of Nazareth, against all the speculations which would create an hiatus, an absolute gulf, between man and God.

No less significant is the controversy over the relation of the divine in Jesus to his human nature. Is he really human, sharing our temptations and sufferings? Or is he just God masquerading in human form? Again Christian intuition triumphs over the subtleties of confused speculation; and Jesus is asserted to be very man of very man, as well as very God of very God. The triumph, however, is nominal, since the emphasis in the Middle Ages upon the supernatural conception of Jesus and the immaculate conception of Mary as "the Mother of God" makes Christianity a miracle play in which God again becomes far removed from fallen man and can be reached only through intermediary beings, the Virgin Mary and the Saints. Mediaeval Christianity had a low conception of the human body. The whole monastic movement is sufficient evidence of that attitude. Theology was solicitous, therefore, to keep God from being soiled by contact with human flesh. Mediaeval theology was concerned with the Eternal Word, not with Jesus of Nazareth.

Since, to the naive imagination of the early Christians, the incarnate presence of God in Jesus ascended to join the Father in the high heavens, and in later theology was translated beyond the temporal world as the Word, or Wisdom of God, eternally present in God, it was necessary that another messenger of God's presence should be conceived as a compensation, lest we be left fatherless. This was provided in the Holy Ghost, the comforter and continuous intercessor, sent from God, or, as a later theology has it, "proceeding from the Father and the Son."[1] The human heart again triumphed over the limitations of its theory by holding to the conviction of the continuous presence of God in human history.[2]

In the Middle Ages, however, this conception of the divine presence was practically institutionalized into the organized Church and its means of grace. The attempt of the Church to express its faith theologically proved a failure. The characteristic doctrines of mediaeval theology became so unintelligible that, towards the end of the Middle Ages, they were gradually removed from the pale of reason. Only the mystical feeling of the real presence of Christ in the Eucharist kept religion vital in the Church.

There is much to admire in mediaeval Christianity. In its missionary zeal it carried the gospel of the fatherhood of God

---

1 The earlier statement was "proceeding from the Father," then the Latin Church added, "and from the Son". This addition was rejected as unorthodox by the Eastern Church and became one of the causes of "the Great Schism" between East and West in the ninth century, A.D.

2 In mediaeval theology the Father becomes power, the Son wisdom and the Holy Ghost love, the bond between the Father and the Son and between God and Man. No wonder the Holy Ghost becomes the centre of the spiritual life.

to the fierce races of Europe, even though this was a sacerdotal and feudal fatherhood. The doctrine of the incarnation was a leaven which must gradually transform the conception of man. Every soul, even the humblest, has immortal value. The Church aimed, within its limitations, to give scope to all the capacities of human nature and to make religion interpenetrate every important function of life. It not only tried to unify the intellectual life of man in scholasticism, but it also gave new meaning to the practical life of man and, through its sanctions, gave stability to society when all else crumbled. It ministered to the emotions in a beautiful devotional liturgy, and it created the Gothic cathedrals, the highest objective expression of the aspirations and mysticism of Christianity that the world has known. They are indeed "sermons in stone." They are the house of God for all the people. In Dante finally a supreme attempt was made to unify the entire life of the age in *The Divine Comedy*. But the Catholic unification was primarily a mystical unification. The sacraments became the vital part, and are still the vital part, of Catholic Christianity.

Chapter Four

THE TRANSITION

Towards the end of the Middle Ages the Church lost its vitality. The very thoroughness of mediaeval organization was its downfall. It became rigid and formal. For the concrete presence of God it substituted an ecclesiastical hierarchy. Loyalty to the Christian ideal of service was sacrificed to an insatiable lust for power. It subordinated conscience to expediency, though there were always sincere voices in the Church that protested against its worldliness. While ecclesiastical intellectualism substituted verbal abstractions for a living reality and thus achieved a statuesque eternity, ecclesiastical mysticism substituted symbols for the spiritual bond and ascribed to these symbols a magic power of their own, or derived from the formula with which they were used, forgetting that the potency of the symbols lies not in themselves but in the living relation which they signify. Its orientation was toward the past rather than toward the future — to stimulate reverence for tradition rather than for the incarnate God, to conserve the past heritage rather than to create a new outlook. It failed to produce a profound impression upon the social life of the time. The chivalry of the Middle Ages was a chivalry of manners rather than a chivalry of democracy. The rigid forms of the Church proved incapable of containing the new soul which was the outgrowth of the spirit that was working in it. By its sharp separation of the spiritual realm, the realm of grace, from the realm of nature, it again left the world adrift and opened the way for the triumph of materialism in a godless world.

In its social conception, the Church of the Middle Ages was modeled upon feudalism — God being conceived as a feudal overlord seated in the high heavens and represented by his vicegerent in Rome. The control which the Church exercised was at best a thin and artificial control — a temporary truce in an internecine conflict, not a durable peace. It served the function of a holding company; it was a transition in a seething, disorganized world. The time had not yet come for the fusion of the various contending factions into a unity of humanity. That time is still far in the future. The chaotic strife of feudalism must precipitate itself first into the more stable equilibrium of nationalism. While the breaking up of an ecclesiastical unity into the many fragments of the Church seems superficially a retrogression, it meant the evolution as a matter of fact of a more thorough and equitable control, and it meant a larger conception of human relations, for the vital control of the Middle Ages had been that of local customs; and the national mind has always tended to progress more rapidly than the local mind. It meant that local customs came under the judgment of the larger national order. The feudal lords became subject to the law of the national sovereign. There came to be one law for the tenant and the squire. After all, the universality of the Middle Ages was a universality largely in name, the colouring was local. That was true of the Catholic Church and of the Holy Roman Empire. The Mediaeval Church lost control, because the social order upon which it was built became defunct. The Church could survive only by adapting itself to new conditions. And it should be said that the Catholic Church has always shown great capacity for adaptation.

When the feudal conception of unity was replaced by national unities, religion tended to become nationalistic. This holds true irrespective of denominations for it is the function of religion to interpret and idealize social relations. The real religion of France has been France, the real religion of Italy has been Italy, the real religion of Britain has been Britain, the real religion of Germany has been Germany. The real religion of

America is America — not merely America as she is, but an America as represented by the idealized personalities of Washington and Lincoln. By the real religion of a people I mean the matrix of customs and ideals which actually controls men's conduct and for which they are willing to fight and to die. In a national crisis, no church can stand if it sets itself against the national will, right or wrong. This shows which is the more vital. In time of war, a nation prays to its God to give it victory against its enemies. And, of course, the enemies make the same prayer to their God. Neither side gives its God any option. The head of the Roman Catholic Church may denounce Naziism, but the Catholic Germans have been praised by Hitler for their bravery in fighting for Nazi Germany. They are first of all Germans. The naked nationalism which shocks us today as Naziism or Fascism is, after all, a logical development of a nationalistic religion which we have camouflaged with Christian phrases. In a time of national danger, we show little respect for individual conscience.

There are indeed signs of a new order. But this order must mean the broadening of the national ideals. It cannot be imposed artificially from outside as was the authority of the Middle Ages. When the nations in the baptism of common danger and in the recognition of a common welfare acquire the consciousness of a common bond, then we shall pray for that welfare; we shall find God incarnated in the new bond. Such a consciousness cannot be sincere while we are practicing imperialism toward nations or races that we deem inferior to ourselves. The new bond must be based upon a new conception and a new feeling for humanity. It cannot rest for long upon a sanction of fear nor can it be merely an alignment of selfish national interests. Meantime the religion of the Nazarene, little understood or realized, is a leaven towards a new order — an order founded upon humanity and not upon the passion for national power and advantage.

The Protestant Reformation did not succeed in liberating the human spirit from bondage to intellectual abstractions and institutional impersonalism. Its theology was modeled upon Augustine and the Middle Ages; and in its organization it merely substituted the king for the pope. While, in its leaders, Protestantism claimed the right to individual interpretation, in fact it merely substituted dogmatic interpretations of the Scriptures for the authority of the Church. It showed little tolerance for divergent interpretations. It soon degenerated into literalism and slavery to creeds, more elaborate and therefore more deadening than the simpler creeds of the Middle Ages. The indiscriminate maintenance of scriptural authority — putting the tribal ethics of the Book of Judges, the vindictive nationalist psalms and the materialistic Ecclesiastes on the same level with the golden sayings of Jesus and of St. Paul — led to the perpetuation of an ethics which is close to the primitive in human nature.[1] It failed in short to return to first things — the gospel of personal relations. God was enthroned afar; and had only an external relation to his world. Human nature was conceived as depraved and impotent. Spirit and mechanism remained in antagonism, with mechanism claiming the world.

The Protestant revolt was nevertheless important and inevitable. Intellectually, it did away with the hierarchy of intermediate beings which had tended to become established in practice in the Middle Ages — the conception of a mediating church, of mediating saints, and of a delegated authority which had made God ever more remote and inaccessible. Protestantism insisted upon the direct accessibility of God and direct responsibility to God, however transcendent God was conceived. The weakness of Protestantism has been its abstractness. It has had little conception of the corporate communion of the Church as

---

1 It would be shocking to Christians and Jews alike to realize how closely Naziism follows the Hebrew tradition of the books of Samuel and the books of Kings, in other words the historical tradition of the Old Testament — a chosen people and the extermination of other peoples and other cultures.

a growing, continuous life, interpreting its traditions in terms
of its needs. It has been primarily intellectualistic. The tendency
has been to put the emphasis on dogmatic interpretation and
to treat the sacraments as accidental rather than as symbols of
the spiritual bond of the faithful. It has given more weight
to doctrine than to the communion of saints, visible and invisible. Catholicism on the other hand has emphasized the
sacramental and institutional aspect. But, instead of regarding
the institution as instrumental to a progressive life, it has
tended to regard the instituion as a thing in itself. Both in their
weakness and in their strength, Catholicism and Protestantism
may be regarded as complementary movements. Both have degenerated from the simple intuition of God as present in
human personal relations. Practically there may be little choice
between an abstract intellectualism and an abstract institution-
alism. The problem is to recover the mystical piety of the
Middle Ages, while maintaining intellectual freedom.

Since in Protestantism intellectual interpretation took the
place of corporate authority, there has been an inherent
tendency to disintegration. It is by virtue of this tendency,
rather than any inherent liberalism, that Protestantism has
offered less inertia to modern thought than Catholicism. If
Christianity rests on individual interpretation and individual
conscience, then it is not obvious why we should be bound
indefinitely by the interpretations of a Luther or a Calvin,
themselves professedly fallible men, however intolerant. New
divisions based on new interpretations of the Scriptures must
arise indefinitely as new leaders arise. Thus Protestantism,
because of its individualism, has become more responsive to
modern tendencies in science and education than its scholastic
sister movement. But it has failed on the whole to adjust itself
in any thoroughgoing manner to modern needs. While pro-
fessing to be Christian, it has clung to the ancient Hebrew
conceptions of personal and national relations. It has made

only a half-hearted attempt to adjust itself to the changes of
modern thought; and even now a considerable proportion of
Protestants remain "fundamentalists," that is, they live intellectually in a pre-Copernican and pre-Darwinian era. While
Catholicism is frankly mediaevalistic, Protestantism halts between two opinions. This condition of things cannot help producing both intellectual and moral insincerity. When Protestantism has become frankly modernistic, it has lost the
sacramental consciousness of religion and has drifted into a
superficial intellectualism and secularism. It has thrown out
the baby with the bath.

We need a religion which shall somehow keep thought alive
while it also ministers to the emotions; which shall encourage
the largest freedom of interpretation while it makes real the
bond of sacramental communion. The old cleavages have out-
lived, it would seem, what usefulness they once may have had
as compensatory movements. A new alignment is called for —
the distinction of progressives and conservatives, those looking
forward and those looking backward, the followers of the
Prophet of reconstruction and the spiritual successors of the
Scribes and Pharisees.

Altogether one cannot help being impressed with the unreality of the religion of today in the more cultured portion
of the population of Protestant countries. There is a lack of
intellectual honesty, on the one hand, and of the spirit of
genuine devotion, on the other. Those who from habit remain
active in the Church are, for the most part, content to repeat
a set of antiquated phrases which were indeed fraught with
significance in their own historic setting — honest attempts to
state religion in terms of human experience then and there —
but which are as foreign to us intellectually as they are inadequate to human relations today. The naturalistic interpretation
of the world dominates the mind of "the intellectuals," whatever concession they may be willing to make to popular reli-

gious prejudice. In any case, God must not interfere with the mechanistic conception of the world. It was the boast of an agnostic orator in the last generation that the time would soon come when the churches would be converted into temples of science. And though we have less confidence in the all-saving power of science today, the wise ones of this world are apt to look upon prayer as a psychological monologue, having at most a certain therapeutic value for the duped believer. But there are more things in heaven and earth than are dreamt of in man's philosophy.

Socially, Protestantism has become a middle class religion. From its inception, Protestantism has been wedded to capitalism. Luther sided against the oppressed peasants in favor of the princes and the landlords; and in Geneva, under the dominance of Calvinism, the foundations of modern capitalism were laid. (In England the class hierarchy was unaffected by the break with the pope.) Protestantism won out among the peoples of northern Europe, because they were restive, individualistic peoples who resented outside control. They believed in thrift and success and they emphasized the good old pagan virtues which go with thrift. These traits were not a result of the theology of early Protestantism which taught the natural depravity and impotence of the individual and his utter dependence upon supernatural grace for the will to any good deed, quite outdoing even Augustine who gave human nature credit for the cardinal pagan virtues, even though he called them "splendid vices." What could have been more deadening to individual initiative then the doctrine of predestination, if people had taken it seriously? It was not the theology of Luther and Calvin which inspired self-reliance but the genius of the people who adopted Protestantism and transformed its theology to meet their demands. Because of the emphasis upon thrift and success, it is easy to see how capitalism became dominant first of all in Protestant countries, and how under free conditions of worship Protestantism came to draw its strength from the middle class. The proletariat, the large industrial class, has largely been left alone by Protestantism except for occasional charity. When the industrial population, with its grime and noisy machinery, moves into the downtown districts, the Protestant churches follow the well-to-do to the suburbs. They have not been greatly concerned about the forty or fifty million industrial toilers of our land. They have not been a great agency for economic reform, as one would expect from the spirit of the Nazarene whom they profess to follow. The result is that the large mass of the proletariat are openly hostile to institutional Christianity and have become willing listeners to the materialistic doctrines of agitators, though sometimes they distinguish between the carpenter Prophet of Nazareth, the friend of the poor and down-trodden, and what seems to them the bourgeois institution that bears his name.

The Roman Catholic church has kept in closer touch with the masses than the Protestant churches. It ministers to all conditions of men, without reference to social status. But it, too, is losing ground. It is bound up historically with the feudal structure of the Middle Ages, which it has faithfully preserved in its own organization and which it has tended to support in modern historical evolution. It has practiced charity toward the poor, but it has not inspired a striving for democracy; and the great democratic revolutions have considered it their enemy. Its official support of the fascistic revolt in Spain, thus placing itself on the side of the feudal landlords and the military caste to the brutal sacrifice of large numbers of its devoted followers, has not tended to establish confidence in its humanity, even though it has since that time denounced the Naziism which crushed Republican Spain. The crushing of the latter was merely the curtain-raiser for the destruction of most of the European democracies. It is true that there are progressive voices both in the Protestant churches and in the Catholic church. But, so far, they are voices crying in the wilderness. They have not affected the economic system, with its inequalities, though the laity of these churches are the controlling part of the system.

You may ask: What does the economic system have to do with the consciousness of the presence of God? The question points to the tragedy of our modern development. Economic values have come to dominate our outlook upon life. The leading idea in capitalistic countries, which are the democratic countries, is that business must be based upon the motive of profit. They have lost, or at least submerged, the idea of business for service. In the totalitarian countries, against which the democracies are fighting for survival, business has been subordinated to the life of the state or a certain type of state. We regard that as an unworthy ideal, but we cannot deny that economic considerations must be subordinated to the larger interests of man. Man is greater than business. Wealth is important but it is not God. It must minister to the welfare of man. The virtues of thrift, so admirable in their proper place, are not the whole of life. They must become instrumental to the spiritual virtues. In a subtle way, capitalism has tended to degenerate into economic materialism. And there is no deadlier enemy of religion. It is all the more dangerous since it may masquerade under religious sanctions. It is an old idea that prosperity is a mark of divine favor. At any rate, the rich have had an undue influence in institutional religion. Jesus used the parable of Dives and Lazarus to point a moral — not that there is virtue in being poor but that the kingdom of heaven cannot be bought. It may be that we all have to be reduced to poverty in order that we may learn that life does not consist in a man's possessions, that the soul is more precious than material things and that the communion of the soul with God is the pearl without price.

If conventional Christianity has failed to meet the problem

of personal relations in our modern life, it has even more conspicuously, if not more really, failed to meet the problem of the relation of national groups. Protestantism has been true on the whole to the tradition of nationalism, namely, that religion follows the flag. No wonder that some nations have drifted into the creed that God is on the side of the strongest battalions and that there is no other right than might. And what can be more pitiable than the futile appeal of the Catholic Church to its children to respect even such decency as is prescribed in past international understandings governing war. Religion can control human conduct only when it interprets the vital relations of human beings to one another and to the universe. And conventional Christianity evidently is failing to do so, and therefore is unheeded. What can such a religion do to reconstruct and heal our shattered world?

The great problem today is to restore the reality of religion in terms of our own life. For the concrete life in religion with its sense of living communion with the unseen, we have substituted abstract words. We have little if any feeling for the reality of God; immortality seems to be a hazy abstraction without potency in our lives; and the communion of saints is likely to seem a bygone superstition. And yet what has our modern wisdom to substitute for the reality which we have lost or to which we have closed the door? "Law is God say some." But I would rather worship a heathen idol than that man-made abstraction which we call law. "Some call it evolution" and bow down and worship it. But the bad in our life is as much evolution as the good. Over such a religion should be inscribed, "in letters of mud," the motto: "Whatever is is right." This would efface all the distinctions of value which make life worth the candle. We must recover the innocence of intuition which, while it

> "Finds tongues in trees, books in the running brooks,
> Sermons in stones, and good in everything,"

yet discriminates between the good and the bad and finds God in the good. We must feel His presence as energizing spirit in all our striving for the best; and He is the best for which we strive — the perfection, the beauty, the goodness which we never reach and yet are the light of all our seeing.

We must wake somehow to the fact that reality above us, around us and in us is more than our dead abstractions which have become our masters. Creative spirit enters in as a real ingredient into our world, and life should be a continuous experiment to attain better things. There is more to the Sistine Madonna than a certain quantitative proportion of pigments. There is the genius, the creative synthesis of the artist, without which the pigments would be a mere daub. It is not likely that the pigments would distribute themselves into a great painting by accident. There is more to the artist's mind that created the painting than a chance collection of chemical elements. There is the spirit of order and beauty. There is more to the universe that produces the artist's mind than the blind dance of atoms. There is the creative, organizing genius that works for order and beauty in our world and inspires in us the impulse to creativeness. Our chemical constituents and their uniformities are not the whole story of reality. They are clay in the hands of the divine potter who shapes them amidst the accidents of the cosmos into some sort of whole. There is more to history than statistical averages. There is the divine energy — ever present, ever creative, giving form to chaos in us and about us. In the long aeons it works to realize something better — always conditioned by the clay in which it works.

The conflict between religion and mechanism is an old and permanent conflict. It dates back to the conflict between religion and magic in primitive religion. The motive of religion has always been to establish personal relations between man and the unseen. It has held steadfastly to the intuition that man, in his fundamental striving and needs, is not an accident in the universe, but that a greater power in the universe stands ready to cooperate with him if he puts himself in right relations to this power. The essence of religion is personal and intimate. Magic, on the other hand, has for its purpose to manipulate the universe by means of formulae that are supposed, on the basis of an uncritical experience, to work. It is void of respect and sympathy for the universe. It substitutes mechanism for personal relations. The inner attitude of the individual becomes irrelevant. It is even so with the modern conception of mechanism, which is the lineal descendant of magic. It looks for formulae with which to predict and control the forces of nature. It would banish personal values from the universe by a wave of the hand as animistic and reminiscent of an unscientific attitude. Ideals are treated as extraneous and fictitious additions to a world conceived as mere matter in motion. But is the mechanical conception of our world the last word? Is the universe which brought us forth indifferent to the higher aspirations which it has implanted in us? Is there not a deeper truth in the saying of Augustine that "God made us for Himself," and therefore the soul can be happy only as it returns to God? Our soul turns to the higher, better portion of the universe as the plant turns to the light.

We have been scared by phrases from claiming the heritage of our whole nature. We have fallen down and worshiped man-made idols — words, formulae, bugaboos of necessity — forgetting that there is more to reality than science can ever hold in its abstractions. The best part — creative spirit, the striving for wholeness — filters through the scientific sieve. We cannot weigh it in our balances, it does not reveal itself to our microscopes. It can be discovered only as it is realized by the creative soul which confronts it. Nor can it be grasped by the intellect alone. It requires also the instincts and emotions — the intimations of our deeper personal life, so mysterious and yet furnishing science its motive and the poet his inspiration. We do indeed need science. We must use it to control our environment. But the end, the feeling for the whole, must come from elsewhere. It is deeper than science. Without it, our scientific abstractions become bricks without mortar, and our scientific ingenuity may be merely a source of mischief. What has science done to unlock the real mystery of things? It has taught us to manipulate, but what about the meaning of it all? One thing is certain, we need more than mere statistical uniformities to account for the potencies, the ideal groping after order, meaning and value which reveal themselves dimly to us. The Spirit still broods over the waters and in the hearts of men. To get the full ingredients of nature's chemistry we must add the organizing Genius of the universe.

Unless we can restore to humanity the sense of living in the presence of God, there is no salvation for civilization. Religion must become a vital part of our life. As with the primitive man, it must include all of life. For nothing can be indifferent to the presence of God. Religion must once more speak with authority in the interpretation of our world. It must not let a philosophy of godless naturalism crowd it from the field of what is most vital to man. But religion can speak with authority only when it interprets what is most real and fundamental in human life. And the most vital question must always be: What does life mean in the last analysis? — which is only another way of asking: What is the relation of our mind and our striving to humanity and the universe of which we are a part?

A great world crisis has exposed our shallowness and our insincerity. It has held up the looking glass to civilization and revealed the brand of Cain. But it has also revealed the deeper need of the human heart. In the stress and strain of life men are looking for something simple and vital — a religion of realities, of mutual helpfulness, instead of words and forms. Is not the difficulty with conventional religion that human souls when they cried for bread were given a stone? That the church instead of leading us into larger unity with man and God has lived in the past? That it has sold its birthright of being the voice of God to the demands of fashion and institutional prosperity? That it has been a blind guide leading the blind — over the precipice? But the day of reckoning has come. The vast mass of struggling human beings is groping for a God who is the friend of man. It feels the need of a new definition of human relations. Institutional Christianity must meet the new problems or go to the wall.

Christianity can make sense again only by going back to first things and by translating afresh its basic intuitions into nobler and more democratic conceptions of the presence of God in man and nature. This is the crucial problem of Christianity today. Christianity must show that God is incarnated, however imperfectly, in our striving for the best and that by following the lead of the best, we shall get a deeper insight into God, the inspirer of the best. This best Christians find embodied in Jesus of Nazareth; but to every man, however humble, when working in sincerity of spirit, grace is given to bring as a gift to the universe his own unique best of truth, beauty and conduct in the relations in which he lives.

The development of the idea of God in human history has been marked, on the one hand, by a continuous tendency towards abstraction and impersonalism, and on the other, by the struggle of the human heart to keep alive, in some way, the sense of real continuity of the human soul with God. The human soul has tried to save itself from a barren intellectualism by various compensatory efforts of imagination. It has been a long struggle to preserve the sense of the real Presence in a world which intellect and custom have made more and more mechanical and soulless. Thus the human heart has created its holy of holies, the doctrine of incarnation, and the Eucharist, to keep the sense of Presence alive and real in the midst of a world of dead abstractions. These compensations are the pro-

test of the mystic against the rationalist; and the human heart
has sided with the mystic. When man loses the consciousness
of the real Presence, religion is dead. When man possesses this
consciousness, his world is transformed into a meaningful
world, whatever may be his picture of the world. But mysticism
is not enough. We require hard and conscientious thinking, as
well as mystical feeling, if we are going to make this a livable
world.

CHAPTER FIVE

CHRISTIANITY AND THE COPERNICAN REVOLUTION

The picture of the world in which Christianity took form was geocentric and anthropocentric. The earth was the stage of the drama of history and man was the climax and end of creation. Dante's *The Divine Comedy* was the culmination of an era. The cosmic order was but the staging of the drama of human destiny — a funnel shaped cavity on one side of the earth for the circles of Inferno, a mountain on the other side for the circles of Purgatory, and spread out above it, in various ranks, the rose shaped Paradise where the petals are the seats of the saints. It was possible in those days for fancy to construct its symbolism, uncontroverted by fact. They were not guilty of the insincerity of trying to reconcile a six day creation with a modern theory of cosmic evolution. They struggled manfully in their own way to meet the problem of evil, not to explain it away. Beset with powers of darkness within and without, they felt comforted by the faith that God could intervene directly in the natural order by His means of grace and thus transform the natural into the spiritual. The forces of nature still seemed subject to control from the realm of the spirit and subservient to supernatural design. It was a smug little world where the sun was appointed to light man by day and the stars by night.

Then came the Copernican revolution in man's scientific picture of nature. The earth was no longer regarded as the center of the universe, but an insignificant part of one small system. The question arose: "What is man that thou art mindful of him and the son of man that thou visitest him?" The earth and man seemed lost in boundless space. The new science proclaimed that this vast universe is governed throughout by mechanical laws. Laplace only voiced the tendency of the new era when he replied to Napoleon that he had found no need of the hypothesis of God in his celestial mechanics. If the Copernican theory made man appear lost in space, so the Darwinian theory made man appear lost in time. Instead of being the summit of creation, man appears as a mere link in the chain of life, the beginning and the end of which are alike lost in mystery. An anthropomorphic religion and an athropomorphic God thus alike appear homeless in the new world of science. The human heart seemed at last to have lost to the intellect in its struggle for the presence of God. The conflict between the new science, supported by exact methods of investigation, and an old theory of the world supported by religious tradition, could have but one outcome — the banishing of the latter. Nor has the new mechanical theory left any loophole for supernatural interference. It fearlessly claims the whole world for its own. And its marvelous success leaves little comfort to those who have tried to support an anthropomorphic religion in the hinterland of science. In the meantime a conventional religion is eking out a precarious existence on the sufferance of science, contenting itself with the crumbs that fall from the rich man's table.

I shall be told that my picture is unnecessarily pessimistic, that science now is becoming idealistic and religious. No doubt some scientists are idealistic and religious. So were Galileo, Kepler and Newton who laid the foundations of modern science. Scientists do not live only by science. They have also their philosophy which may or may not have any relation to their science. It is true that revolutionary conceptions have come into science in the twentieth century. Such conceptions as the electron, the quantum of radiation, theories of relativity, have had profound influence upon the science of our day. But I cannot see how these conceptions, as used by science, are, on the face of them, more idealistic than the older conceptions which they have replaced. The indeterminacy of the electron (if it is indetermined) does not make it more spiritual. There is nothing of value in mere chance. The laws of quantum mechanics, which are conceived as statistical averages (like insurance tables), are no more spiritual than the classical laws of physics which had already taken the statistical form. It is a difference in mathematics which the layman cannot follow. Theories of relativity have to do with measurements within the space-time perspectives of moving masses in space, not with relation to our ideals. Einstein's theory of gravitation substitutes a new and more difficult set of equations for the Newtonian theory, but the conception of gravitation as due to the curvature of space in the neighborhood of matter is as physical as the Newtonian conception of direct attraction of bodies upon one another according to the law of the inverse square. Neither conception brings us nearer to God, however strong the religious feeling of Newton or Einstein.

It is a great mistake on the part of the modernists to substitute science for religion. On the other hand, a religious view of the world cannot, for long, incorporate an antiquated science. In this respect the Catholic church has shown its historic wisdom. After fighting the Copernican theory for generations, it discovered that the new astronomy did not affect the fundamental values of Christianity which therefore could be translated into the new language of science. After fighting Darwinism with all its strength, it discovered that its own master theologian, St. Thomas Aquinas, had already furnished the key to a new interpretation, namely, that the Creative Genius in the universe proceeds by steps and gradations from the simplest to the highest. (St. Thomas would have said from the highest to the simplest.) We must think of God as ever creative. Evolution and creation are but different points of view. Evolution is description, creation is interpretation. Science describes the body, not the Soul of Nature. Its usefulness lies in its abstractness, but just, therefore, its truth must be supplemented by poetry and religion.

It cannot be denied that a crisis confronts the religious interpretation of the universe. That it will win out in the end is as certain as that it is fundamental in human nature. But this will involve a radical reinterpretation of religion, on the one hand, and of science on the other. Each has its claims, and in so far as the claims are genuine there is no real conflict. That the world lends itself to the naturalistic interpretation of science is as clear as it is useful. But the religious interpretation of the world remains a vital demand of the human soul, for if the universe has no meaning, science itself can have no meaning. Those who, with the author of Psalm 139, feel the divine guidance both in the vast spaces and in the genetic process have no need to worry about the revolutions in science.

The poet and the philosopher have attempted to do what the theologian has failed to do, namely, to interpret the Copernican universe so as to make the soul with its demands feel at home in the new world of thought. According to pantheistic idealism there is no fundamental difference between matter and mind. What seems matter to us is but mind, "hide-bound with habit." Really, there moves a soul in the whole; and the order of nature is but another way of looking at the order of the universal mind. Every part of the universe is therefore a revelation, however fragmentary, of the operations of the infinite Spirit; and the world of the senses is but the sign language of the mind of God. God, says pantheistic idealism, is not far from you: He is in you, He is you, if you only understand yourself.

> "They reckon ill who leave me out;
> When me they fly I am the wings."

There is but one ultimate reality and that is the mind of God. All our thinking and searching moves in God — is God's becoming conscious of Himself in us.

The gulf between the world of nature and the world of grace, which was the outcome of mediaeval thought, is thus abolished. The conflict between the Copernican view of the universe and the religious view has disappeared. There is but one order and that is the divine order. Nature is no longer conceived as a game of chance. Nature is the home of God, his revelation. In the beautiful lines of Wordsworth:

> "For I have learned
> To look on nature, not as in the hour
> Of thoughtless youth, but hearing oftentimes
> The still sad music of humanity:
> Nor harsh nor grating though of ample power
> To chasten and subdue. And I have felt
> A presence that disturbs me with the joy
> Of elevated thoughts; a sense sublime
> Of something far more deeply interfused,
> Whose dwelling is the light of setting suns,
> And the round ocean and the living air,
> And the blue sky, and in the mind of man:
> A motion and a spirit that impels
> All thinking things, all objects of all thought,
> And rolls through all things."

The human heart has thus turned a veritable *coup d'état* against its enemies. It has triumphed over mechanism and materialism at a moment when these seemed in supreme control and has proclaimed the pervasive and inclusive presence of God. Yet the victory seems too easy and too sweeping. The romantic idealism of the first half of the nineteenth century was a reaction from the mechanistic materialism of the eighteenth century and like all compensatory movements emphasized the other extreme. It thus "o'erleaped itself and fell on the other," and so we have the naturalism of the later nineteenth and of the first part of the twentieth century. Extremes have a way of meeting. Hegelian idealism became Marxian materialism. But this oscillation between monistic materialism and monistic spiritualism solves no problems. Matter and spirit each has its claim. And we shall not magnify the claims of spirit by denying the claims of matter. Spirit requires matter as its instrument. Matter requires spirit as its end. The conception of God which makes Him the traveler and the path, the slayer and the slain, the tempter and the tempted deprives individual life of reality and makes the drama of history a farce. God wilfully dupes Himself in a game of hide and seek with Himself. Such a conception works a strain upon our moral consciousness which in a great crisis of the soul makes it monstrous. We cannot say in the words of Tennyson:

> "Our wills are ours we know not how,
> Our wills are ours to make them Thine."

For in the world of pantheistic idealism there can be no "we" in an ultimate sense. There can be no "wills" but God's. God is merely carrying on a monologue with Himself. In such a world it would hold indeed that "the good is perfect and the bad is just as perfect," which is repugnant to all that is best within us. Rather does our moral consciousness side with the ancient prophet: "Woe to them that call good evil and evil good."

It was Plato, the greatest of idealists, who pointed out that God must not be conceived as "the cause of all things, but of the good only, and not the cause of evil." We need a selective God — a God who is not merely a name for things as they are, but who stands and works for things as they ought to be. To quote Plato again: "God, if He be good, is not the author of all things, as the many assert, but He is the cause of a few things only, and not of most things that occur to men; for few are the goods of human life, and many are the evils, and the good only is to be attributed to Him: of the evil other causes have to be discovered." And "the good is the advantageous," "the cause of well-being," not a mere abstraction. How much mischief has been done in human history by false conceptions of God! We must insist with Plato that "God is always to be represented as he truly is, perfectly simple and true both in deed and word, the fairest and best that is conceivable." The God we shall worship must indeed be more than a tribal God, more than a national God, more even than the God of our little earth. He must be a pervasive and effective presence in the entire world order to guarantee the things that are really worth while. He is the God of the whole universe uniting all the worshipers in one bond, because He is the common good and the triumphant good in the universe. He lightens our darkness. He brings order out of the chaos of our purposes in some fashion, and in this creative work we may have a part. But God is not the whole of things. Blindness and maladjustment are real and tragic facts in our world, and need to be cured.

No problems are solved by calling everything God. The hydra-headed monster of evil still remains under a more euphonious name.

> "The wrong that pains my soul below,
> I dare not throne above,"

sang the Quaker poet, Whittier. The demand must always be for a force working for righteousness and beauty in our motley world, for some Prometheus who at the cost of infinite pain is striving to introduce a new order, spite of maladjustment and selfishness. Pantheistic idealism, like its opposite, monistic materialism, destroys the scale of values. Practically it identifies God with things as they are. The difference between pantheistic idealism and materialism becomes practically a difference in name, as Feuerbach so clearly saw. All you need is emergent evolution and presto! Matter changes into life and mind. What we need is not a God who is everything and does everything, but a God who stands for ideals, who, in spite of the inertia and the limitations, set by blindness and accident in the finite struggle of our world, strives to come to expression in history, who hallows our sacrifice, who condemns our egoism, who stimulates our courage and earnestness, and also our sense of humor amidst the petty incongruities of experience, and who shares not only our suffering but also our joy of life — a God who makes it worth while to work and fight and die.

Pantheistic idealism, even when invested with poetic beauty, fails to meet our needs. But we cannot go back to the anthropomorphic religion of the past. It is impossible for an anthropomorphic God to do the business of a Copernican universe. He could not even do the wholesale business, let alone doing the retail business of personal attention to the infinite details of such a world as this. Our religious imagination, with its ancient symbols, stands bankrupt before the new conception of the world. And the consciousness of the impotence of our religious ideas cannot help having a paralyzing effect upon our emotions and conduct. No wonder that the world of religion has come to seem a sideshow to a material universe and that naturalism and mechanism have come to dominate the minds of cultured men. Even if a partnership of such a world and an anthropomorphic God is admitted, it means necessarily a patronizing attitude to God. We are where the ancient world was in the last stage of its civilization when Lucretius consigned the gods to the superspaces as perfect but impotent spectators of a mechanical world. And it must be noted that a religion which fails to minister to the minds of the thinking part of the population cannot long hold the confidence of the masses. Ancient civilization failed to work out its problem. It plunged into mysticism and eventually was supplanted, in the general chaos of a humanity-in-the-making, by a simpler religion and a less sophisticated civilization which now in turn stands at the same cross-roads. Has our religion the capacity to reorganize itself or must it go under?

If the conventional conception of God has proved incapable of meeting the intellectual demands of modern life, so has it equally failed to meet the practical needs. The conception of God as a patriarchal landlord or a feudal king has been as impotent to meet the new social problems as to meet the new conception of the universe. It has, on the contrary, been the bulwark of an antiquated social order from which we are striving so desperately to liberate ourselves. The Copernican change from capitalistic feudalism to a universal democracy, with equal opportunity for every man, woman and child, is as incompatible with our traditional religion as is the change from the geocentric to the cosmic point of view. In both respects institutional religion must set its house in order. If it was the insincerity of popular religion which made a world catastrophe possible, will humanity be satisfied for long with a religion which repeats the somnolent phrases of a dead social order? Will they continue to consign religion to the women and children while they go about their business until overtaken by another catastrophe? There are worse things in store for mankind than fascistic dictatorship if it fails to take the present condition as a warning to wholehearted reform, intellectual and moral.

We need a real reformation — a reformation which shall be more than a change of external forms. We need a reformation which shall translate Christianity into the tissue of the vital thought and striving of today — into terms of creative energy instead of static being, into terms of genuine democracy instead of industrial feudalism. We need a thoroughgoing religion — a religion which shall define man's true place in the universe, a religion which shall include all of life. The separation of religion from this world has led to a cynical materialism in the real affairs of life and has made religion a merely technical matter. We cannot afford to continue a compartmental view of life. Away with a religion which preaches "business is business," "politics is politics," "art for art's sake." Such an attitude means that higher ideals have no place in the practical dealings of men. It means that self-interest and expediency become the dominant motives of individuals and nations. It was against such a conception of religion that the great prophets of Israel inveighed with all their might. Such a religion must lead to dissolution as of old. It lacks the cement to hold human society together. We need a religion which preaches business for the sake of the community, politics for the sake of better social relations, art and science for humanity's sake. Religion should envelop life from beginning to end in a sane, healthful and devout atmosphere. It should initiate the life of the individual into the social faith into which he is born and of which he is the promise, but it should not forget to work for the promise of a new order. It should unify and consecrate all of life's activities through an ideal of the common good. Our conception of God must be broad enough to be the ideal and fulfillment of all that is noble and worthy in human nature. Our concepts must be remade to express the relation of God to our twentieth century activities and needs. We have failed to heed the warning that new wine must have new bottles, and we are spilling the wine. Christian theology has been stereotyped for over a thousand years. It is time that it should interpret and idealize what men live by. It would be better for Christianity to be, as it once was, a small persecuted society, if thus it might be a genuine leaven for righteousness, rather than that it should rest in a nominal acceptance through being compounded with the selfish interests of this world. The real followers of the idealism of Jesus have always been a small number and have always seemed visionaries from the point of view of this world.

The question has been raised: "Has Christianity failed? And the answer has been made: "It has not been tried." But why has it not been tried? The Christian church has been in existence nineteen hundred years. If it had been animated by the idealism of the Master whom it professes to follow, if it had preserved the zeal and the willingness to sacrifice which the early church possessed, could it then be said that Christianity has not been tried? One thing is certain, the church has failed. To become a vital factor of regeneration it must recover the intuition of the Master, of the real presence of God. For meaningless worn-out phrases, it must substitute sincerity and truth. It must acquire a new orientation as regards social relations both as regards the relations of nations and as regards the relations of persons. Of the two, the latter is indeed the more fundamental, for a true conception of personal relations must reflect itself in true group relations. The church must become the church of all the people, the church of humanity. What an irony of history that a church which was the hope of the poor and oppressed, of the proletariat, should have come to seem the bulwark of special privilege. Finally the church must reorganize itself as an institution. It must become conscious of its real purpose and reshape itself to express that purpose more effectively. How can a feudal church express the gospel of democracy? How can a church divided by jealousy and intolerance express Christian unity? It is not necessary that the various denominations should sacrifice their traditions or cults so far as these genuinely minister to the varieties of human nature. Let each enrich the whole with its gifts, but let there be clear recognition and friendly cooperation in the one purpose — to make the world better.

There is one article of faith which has reality for some of us today and that is democracy. For the dream of democracy, nations in an hour of crisis, have put forth their collective strength. For it millions have made and are making the supreme sacrifice. But let us firmly resolve not to repeat the mistake of the recent past: No sooner was the crisis over than the old forces of selfishness and greed were found to be still in the saddle. The battle for genuine democracy is still to be won, and it will be a long and bitter struggle before we shall win the liberty of man, woman and child. Democracy must become a religion if it is to succeed — not a religion of lip service which we have now, but a genuine devotion to the ideal of the Nazarene, the infinite worth of every individual. This would be a moral Copernican revolution. We cannot divide nations into good and bad nations. All have sinned. All must learn to recognize the mutual human claims. We boast of democracy. But what sort of democracy is it where one third of the population is on the verge of starvation? Every age has its own problem of social reconstruction. As the problem of the Renaissance was national emancipation and the problem of the eighteenth and nineteenth centuries was individual emancipation, so the problem today is international and industrial reconstruction.

The great problem of today is to liberate man from the machinery of civilization, to make the machine an instrument instead of a master. We have become slaves of the machinery of words, of phrases. We must remake our phrases to express our real experience and thus infuse into them a living soul. We have become slaves of the machinery of institutions. We must reorganize our institutions so that they may become the true body of our collective soul, instead of cramping our souls within outgrown forms. It seems to be the fate of man that no sooner has he created an institution than the child enslaves its parent. We have become the slaves of the machinery of industrialism. We must make the machinery of the new industrialism, whether the machinery of the plant or the machinery of organization, serve the needs of man, of human development and happiness. The great problem, in short, is to save our soul from the Frankenstein that our civilization has erected, to vindicate the values of first-hand human relations.

We are in the midst of one of the great crises in history. Again, the battle cry is Freedom. No people that is not willing to sacrifice and die for its freedom can long remain a free people. They have already confessed that they are slaves and the conqueror will soon make this slavery a fact. Youth again is sacrificing itself heroically on many battlefields *against* the enemies of democracy. But we can not win a real victory by merely fighting *against* something. We must fight *for* something. If the democracies are to survive they must furnish the substance and not merely the appearance. Freedom must not be merely a slogan of war, but the opportunity to realize the good life for all mankind. We must see to it that the youth of the world is not sacrificed in vain a second time. While we are fighting the enemies of human freedom abroad, let us not forget the traitors in our midst, those who would maintain the old order of inequality and exploitation. Let us fight for humanity at home as well as abroad.

PART TWO

THE CREATIVE PRESENCE

CHAPTER SIX

THE REDEFINITION OF GOD

We have seen that the abstract idea of God is the result of the abstract use of language. The effect of this has been to substitute words for realities. We have killed the sense of intuition of the immediate living relation and substituted abstract definitions. If our speculative idea of God, dressed up with a long list of abstract attributes, comes to us from mediaeval theology, our popular conception comes to us from the mediaeval painter. We can see now the wisdom of the second commandment in the Hebrew decalogue with its strong injunction against any images or likenesses whatsoever of Jehovah. The anthropomorphic images, handed down from the Middle Ages, have done a great deal to stereotype Christianity in people's minds. It must be recognized, however, that the pictures by the mediaeval painters of the Trinity, of the Madonna and the Christ child, and of the mediating saints have had a historic value in their attempt to bridge the gulf of abstraction and to make a distant God seem somehow accessible. They served a function in the childhood of a new culture. But they also served to perpetuate a stage which man in his maturity must outgrow. When did God, who in the days of the patriarchs was felt to walk with man, ever move away into the high heavens? The ancient psalmist has a better version:

"Whither shall I flee from thy presence? Or whither shall I go from thy spirit? If I ascend into heaven, thou art there: If I make my bed in hell, behold thou art there. If I take the wings of the morning, and dwell in the uttermost parts of the sea, even there shall thy hand lead me, and thy right hand shall hold me. If I say, surely the darkness shall cover me, even the night shall be light about me. Yea, the darkness hideth not from thee; but the night shineth as the day: the darkness and the light are both alike to thee. For thou hast possessed my reins; thou hast covered me in my mother's womb." If religion shall become a real factor in human life, it must bring afresh the intuition of the creative presence of God. Christianity has done well to emphasize that presence in Jesus of Nazareth, but we need to become conscious of that presence in the life of today.

We need to return to clear thinking and honest conviction in religious matters. The blame is not on early Christianity. It struggled manfully to translate Christianity into a world of Greek concepts and Roman institutions and succeeded so well that it conquered the ancient world. Nor is the blame on the mediaeval Church. It wrought with a solemn sincerity and mastered the entire fabric of mediaeval civilization which it heightened and unified; and thus became the controlling factor in the life of its time. The trouble is with us that we are repeating the phrases of past thinking without thinking for ourselves. We are failing to translate Christianity into the concepts and institutions which are characteristic of our day. Hence Christianity is failing to guide the life of its own followers; and it is failing to lend a helping hand to other civilizations which are in the process of reconstruction. It is failing today as a missionary religion in Africa and the Orient, while Mohammedanism is extending its influence with astounding rapidity. The Orient has indeed accepted our science, our medicine, our

education, and even our social and political ideas; but it fails
to find reality in our religion. Christianity does not interpret
the needs of today and therefore does not speak with conviction. As the early church constructed its own theology in terms
of the civilization of its day, and mediaeval religion dared to
construct its theology to meet the needs of the time, so we
must construct a theology which interprets our own period of
development.

We must make over our theology, which is merely the scaf-
folding of the inner life, to conform to the concepts and relations which are vital today. In mediaeval theology, God was
conceived as being, the source of existence, though the abstract
logical concept of being was suffused with mysticism. God was
conceived as including all predicates within Himself. Upon this
conception is based the famous argument of Anselm for the
existence of God. If God includes all attributes, if He is the
most real being, then He must of course include existence.
Naturally this conception tended toward pantheism, since there
could be no reality outside of God. God became *the* substance.
But what strikes one is the purely formal character of this
conception of aseity or self-existence when thus reduced to
cold words. We are dealing with definitions. We do not feel
that we have gotten nearer to the reality of things. Today
instead of speaking in terms of being or substance we speak
in terms of energy — pervasive energy which is present everywhere by its activity. This, for us at least, becomes a more fruitful way of thinking. It is no longer necessary to identify God
with the whole of things. Rather is He that creative energy,
that spiritual power that works for the good, — a leaven, a
catalytic agent which works constructively in our world for
order, unity, and harmony. And while we cannot say that everything is in God, we can say that God is present everywhere
by His essence and power. Just because God's activity is in
the direction of development, selective of that which is whole-

some and normal as contrasted with the destructive tendencies in our world, therefore individuals and groups must tend towards harmony with God or commit suicide. At any rate, the relation to a God who is living, pervasive, intelligent moral energy, a constructive mind working for ideals in the universe, makes an appeal for life and cooperation that the mere idea of self-existence does not make. It makes creation a present and real fact. It is true that there is the idea of continuous creation in mediaeval theology, but it has no meaning for us when coupled with the idea of God as a timeless, self-sufficient being. If God is outside of time, if we are not part of His creative realization, then life and history have no meaning.

We feel today that the proof for the existence of God must be based upon human experience and not upon formal definitions. If anything comes to the creative mind with overwhelming force, it is the consciousness that the emergence in man of creative impulse, and the ideals which come to light through it, must somehow be of a piece with the universe which produced it and not the accident of blind chance. It is because there is an intelligent direction in the universe, a Genius working for ideals, that the universe, in its creative trial-and-error adaptation, evolves the organization which in us becomes conscious of order and works to create order. A mind which does not have this consciousness of continuity with its source is debauched by dead abstractions.

The idea that God is *one* follows in speculative theology from the concept of God as the inclusive being. But this has never made any practical appeal to the lay mind. The difficulty of thinking of God as abstract unity is evidenced by the trinitarianism of traditional Christianity. According to this theology God manifests Himself in three modes or persons, — Father, Son and Holy Spirit. This has indeed its historic significance in man's attempting to preserve as real for himself the presence of God. When the human heart became conscious of the presence of God in Jesus of Nazareth, the abstract intellect gave this presence a name and conceived it as a numerically separate person, and when in turn the human heart recognized the continuity of the Spirit of truth and goodness in human life even after the death of Jesus, the abstract intellect must perforce erect this presence into a third person. But it has always been difficult to hold together the abstract numerical attributes of unity and trinity, and the non-Christian world has always challenged the monotheism of orthodox Christianity. There can be no doubt that in the popular consciousness, with the pictures of the painter in mind, the trinity was more real than the unity.[1] In any case numerical metaphors must be inadequate to the richness of the life of God.

That the traditional symbolism of the trinity has served a genuine purpose, there can be no doubt. Else it could not have persisted through the centuries. The doctrine of the trinity was a compensatory device to correct the abstract deism which was the background of Christianity. Here has lain its appeal. An intellectualistic unitarianism has failed to appeal to the Christian world to any considerable extent. Nor can this be explained by a difference of intellectual culture or of mental capacity, since orthodox Christianity has included some of the greatest minds of the centuries. It can be accounted for only by the fact that the confused and antiquated concept of trinitarianism hides a sound intuitive need. The human soul, first of all, demands personal relations with the creative goodness of the universe, — a master mind responding to our minds, encouraging and strengthening them in all noble activity, and at the same time making intelligible the creative process which brought our mind into existence. An impersonal constitution or inclusive logical system, such as intellectualism has attempted, has failed to meet our religious needs. Christian tradition, further, empha-

---

1 While speculative theology conceived the distinctions of the trinity as hypostases, personae, "masks," of the one essence, the popular imagination pictured them as separate individuals.

sizes the infinite value and potentiality of personality, and Jesus has furnished, as no one else, the ideal and embodiment of personal worth. Hence the faith in the unique incarnation of divinity in Jesus, and potentially at least in personality everywhere. This is expressed in the concept of the universal fatherhood of God and the moral equality and brotherhood of man. Finally, there is the conviction that God is continually incarnated in human history — in individuals and in groups, so far as they permit —; and that all cooperative endeavor for truth, right and beauty is a manifestation of His guiding, creative spirit — not limited by ecclesiastical councils, though these may embody, as the council of Nicaea did, the wisdom of an age, but always present in the spiritual succession of those consecrated to the holy cause of humanity. We must respect the intuition which underlies orthodox Christianity; but we must strive to bring it into the light of day by expressing it in concepts which are part of our present thinking and social insight.

We must indeed think of God as unity in the sense of meaning a direction of activity, a Spirit guiding toward that ideal which we can but faintly grasp, but which must give worth to the motley changes of the universe. God is not an abstract unity, apart from the creative variety of His activity. We see here again the effect of verbal abstraction. We give the energies that reveal themselves as light a name, and we speak and think of light as one thing. It is indeed a type which we can recognize and distinguish from other energies, but what makes it real is its infinite variations, — never the same on the placid mirror of the sea and on the troubled waters, shifting all the time in endless detail with the variation of the medium and the refracting surface. So we call mind one. It is indeed a type of activity. The well organized mind has a direction which we can identify and with which we can establish practical relations. But it is only a stereotyped mind which acts in only one way. The mind of genius reveals itself in endless variety, — new surprises, unique creative acts in which the development of genius is made manifest. So we give the divine energy a name and call it one, and it is one directive Genius, yet it is the infinite variety of God's activity which reveals the richness of his reality rather than the abstract unity of type.

We speak of God as eternal, as the same yesterday, today, and forever. It is true that God always stands for the best. He is the goal of our striving, the eternal object of our loyalty. We therefore can depend upon Him in our striving for the best. He is always ready, moreover, to help us in our efforts toward better living. But this does not mean that the divine mind is stereotyped, that God has passed into senility, as the mediaeval painters have impressed upon us. Rather God is eternal youth. He is ever reborn in the drama of history, and it is in His reincarnation that we know Him. All that we know of goodness and perfection in our own experience has the character of growth, of infinite development. And however inadequate our experience, it must ever be the door to the higher reality. We must believe that God is ever creative; that His genius finds ever new expression in a changing, moving world; that His life is a cumulative drama of new activity, new discovery, new fulfilment, an evergrowing unity of purpose, striving in the infinite changes of the universe to realize the best.

The old theology has spoken of God as omnipresent. This was derived again from God as the inclusive being. Rather is God present as light is omnipresent, — except where our opaqueness excludes Him, — always waiting at the threshold to enter in, incarnated in all our endeavors for the best. In the beautiful words of Tennyson:

"Speak to Him, thou, for He hears, and
spirit with spirit can meet —
Closer is He than breathing and
nearer than hands and feet."

God is present as opportunity for achievement in mind and character, — not to be attained without preparation and co-operation on our part, but as an inspiration for the best, a democratic opportunity in the sense that it is not limited to caste or station but open to Epictetus, the slave, as to Marcus Aurelius, the Emperor, yea to Mary Magdalene and the thief on the cross.

Once we conceive God as a pervasive energy stimulating toward the best, we get a new light on the ontological attributes. God is not omnipresent in the sense of including everything, since we can shut him out from our souls by our perverse habits of thought and action. We can make ourselves opaque to God. He is not omnipotent in the sense that He can do everything, for He can do no evil. The mediaeval conception of omnipotence was bought at the expense of the reality of finite wills. In its inexorable logic, as worked out by Augustine and Calvin, history is made the mere staging of an eternal plan, a puppet show in which the salvation or damnation of the individual is seen as part of the eternal plot of history. The damned too contribute to the perfection of the whole. A painting requires shadow as well as light, tragedy requires a villain. Such a conception becomes revolting when one contemplates that all the misery, injustice, and cruelty of the world would be part of the eternal scheme. The abstract idea of omnipotence makes a mockery of the goodness and justice of God. Rather must we conceive of God as limited in His effectiveness by our willingness, by our cooperation or opposition. Our attitude makes a real difference to God's activity. And while God, because his activity means the wholesome, the economic and best, both in human and cosmic evolution, must win out in some fashion, the character of the result is conditioned by our activity. Our attitude must necessarily affect our part in the whole, and in the intimate interrelations of life it is bound to affect a great deal more than that. We

may figure in the world picture as shadow rather than light
and thus affect the harmony of the whole; but at any rate we
have something to say as to how we figure, and God is justified.
In the world of our moral consciousness God must wait upon
our decisions. Our choices alter the constitution of the universe,
they are not the rehearsal of an old tale. And while God, like
a master chess player, can foresee our possible moves, he must
wait for the outcome and make his own moves accordingly.

We must be careful, however, not to dogmatize about the
mind of God. We have been too intellectualistic in our conception of God in the past. We have been too prone to assume
that we were thinking God's thoughts after Him or for Him.
We have been too ready to make a logic machine of God.
It is possible that He may have ways of perceiving and com-
prehending our world that infinitely pass ours — more sensitive
than the camera film, more comprehensive in His intuitions of
relations than our slow thought can fathom. Nor is His thought
a mere abstract verbal relation to things. His is creative intelligence. While "he sees all over, thinks all over, hears all over,"
what is more important is that He enters into creative relations
with our world to produce order, goodness, and beauty. This
relation is more than interpenetration, more than intussuscep-
tion: it is a new creation, a new birth in grace and beauty.
We cannot, as finite, be of "one essence with the Father" but
the essence of God is present everywhere and always, and by
being compounded with the divine energy, we emerge as a
new and higher unity of life.

The juristic idea of God has dominated Christian theology.
Hymnology, which is popular theology, is full of the idea. If
it is no longer the ransom of the human soul from the devil,
the death of Jesus is still conceived by some as the satisfaction
of the demands of the implacable justice of God. We have
conceived love and justice as abstract attributes, having no com-
merce with each other. God, therefore, must give with one hand

to satisfy the other, the implication being that the left hand does not know what the right hand does. If God's justice means the exaction of the full pound of flesh, then the bloody sacrifice must of course be provided. And since man could not pay the debt or even interest, some one else must pay it to restore normal relations. But was God ever an implacable judge, incapable of forgiveness? This is hardly the idea of a loving father unless we return to the primitive period of human sacrifice. Can one wonder that sound, intelligent human beings turn away from a God who is pictured as worse than themselves? The Hebrew psalmist gives us another version: "Like as a father pitieth his children, so the Lord pitieth them that fear him. For he knoweth our frame; he remembereth that we are dust." We have transferred our wooden machinery of justice into the economy of God. We place men in abstract classes as good or bad, yet to a being of infinite discernment there must be much that is bad in the best of us and much that is good in the worst of us, and we are all in need of redeeming love. It is not consistent with what we know of Jesus that he regarded it as his chief function to be a sacrifice to meet the demands of outraged justice nor can we accept this as a fitting interpretation of his death. Rather is it the survival of the feudal order of the Middle Ages, — as honest and relevant in its own setting as it is anachronous today. The chief contribution of Jesus, we believe, is that he discovered and made real the presence of God in himself and in others, — a God who is ever ready to receive and to help his groping children. There is indeed vicarious sacrifice and the world is being redeemed through such sacrifice, — the mother's vicarious sacrifice that love may go on, Jesus' sacrifice to raise men to their higher potentialities, the sacrifice which the pioneers of progress must always make. But theirs is a sacrifice of love, not for abstract justice, but that love may conquer over selfishness and hate, that the world may be made a better world. We have

gotten over the idea of retributive justice in our penology. It is
time we were getting over it in religion. I believe that Portia's
conception of justice represents Christianity rather than
Shylock's:

> "The quality of mercy is not strained,
> It droppeth as the gentle rain from heaven
> Upon the place beneath
>
> .   .   .   .
>
> And earthly power does then show likest God's
> When mercy seasons justice."

On the other hand, the conception of God as all mercy,
whose chief function is to forgive sins and in whose economy
right character and right doing are of no importance is equally
revolting to our moral sense. This idea is the complement of the
feudal conception of a vicarious sacrifice, a payment once for
all for the sins of the world, past, present, and future. This
conception has been emphasized *ad nauseam* by sentimental
Protestantism. Such an idea of God's relation to man would
free the individual from responsibility and all that would be
necessary would be passive acceptance. The difficulty with the
traditional conception of justice and of love is that they are
abstract and independent attributes, while in reality God's relations are personal — a justice and a love which have to do
with struggling temporal human beings in their personal and
group relations. God loves clean living and high thinking.
Love and justice are not abstract, separate characteristics in
God or in man. God's love, like true human love, is a regenera-
tive force which purifies and makes men good. It is not a stereotyped wholesale love, a gift once for all, any more than a
mother's love for her children is stereotyped and wholesale.
As the mother loves each child in a unique way, having reference to its potentialities and its development, so we may
imagine that God loves the world. But God being a just, true,
loyal God cannot love injustice, treachery and dishonor whether
in groups or individuals. Nor can He forgive them any more

than we can forgive them, while that is their attitude. "The soul that sinneth he shall die," holds of individuals and groups, as truly as it holds that if they repent and turn themselves to better ways they shall live. God never wills the death of the sinner. His property is always to have mercy. Language and custom have tended to make up God of abstract, contradictory attributes, but God is a harmonious life, not a sum of attributes. The contradiction is in our awkward logic.

We must remember, moreover, that there is more to God than we can comprehend or state in any formulae. It is dogmatism which is irreverent in that it degrades God to the level of a certain stage of man's comprehension. We must not apply our measure, numerical or moral, to God; but must at the same time try to understand God in every age in His relations to us and to our needs. And we must remember that His relation varies with our needs as the relation of the parent to the child varies with its development. God's relation to an individual or an age is always real and vital, then and there. Our definitions have a value in so far as they are helpful in our relations to one another, but they are always provisional and must give way to conceptions which express those relations in a more mature stage of development. They are at best the light breaking to-usward and coloured by our experience. There are, however, two qualities which seem particularly divine as we find them in human life — one is loyalty to the best as God gives us to see the best, the other is the openmindedness to experiment in order to find the best, and the readiness to make it our own from wheresoever it may come.

One thing is certain, that a religion in order to be vital at any one time must express itself in the matrix of living human relations at that stage of development. That a nomad people should find God as the chief shepherd, that a patriarchal people should express God as father, that a theocratic monarchy should think of God as its real king, that a people brought up in the tradition of sacerdotalism and priestly sacrifices should interpret God and Jesus in terms of its priestly ritual, that a feudal organization should state its relation to God in terms of feudal chivalry and justice, that a narrow nationalism should think of God as following the flag — all this was normal and made religion a real fact at the time. But that Christianity today should persist in expressing itself in life-relations which have been outgrown, this is disloyal and abnormal. No wonder traditional Christianity has lost its power to guide and control human beings. It does not speak to them in terms of their actual life. We need a religion which shall express the meaning of the striving for democracy and a broader humanity, — a religion for which there shall be neither Jew nor Gentile, neither Greek nor barbarian, neither male nor female, neither slave nor free, but humanity striving to realize itself in a common bond. Our old moulds of political organization have proven too narrow and are endangering the fruits of civilization and the very life of the race. We must have a broader conception of human relations which shall conserve but sublimate the smaller units into a larger moral federation. This cannot come to pass unless our religious prophets lead the way. It must be a union consecrated in the faith of God to withstand human selfishness — only more dangerous when it is the selfishness of groups. We need a religion which shall lead the way in the upward striving of the large mass of humanity for greater freedom and opportunity. Failing this we are likely to land in a social anarchy and internal strife worse than any external war between groups.

In the midst of this world upheaval we need a return to Jesus of Nazareth, the friend of everyman, the champion of humanity wherever found. We need His consciousness of the presence of God; we need that willingness to sacrifice for others that his life and death exemplify. Nothing could so well express the meaning of his life and his conception of God as a truly democratic society — the door of opportunity open to all, the divine incentive to strive for the highest excellence that we may be the servant of all. To this end we need to remove the encrustations of centuries of interpretation. We must return to the simple intuition of a God present in human life, and in the world about us, a God energizing and inspiring all worthy motives, a God, immanent in the sense that he sustains creative relations to us, transcendent in that He is more than we, — infinitely better than our best and therefore setting an ideal for our striving — personal in that He enters into creative communion with us and participates with us in our striving for the best.

CHAPTER SEVEN

GOD AS CREATIVE ENERGY

In order to understand the life in religion, we must take it in concrete life situations, not as verbal abstractions. The abstractions of science and the abstractions of theology are alike deadening. They lead to the same result — mechanism and materialism. For a mechanical God is as indifferent to our personal fortunes as is mechanical matter. We need to think of God in new terms, — new metaphors, if you like, for, after all, our thinking is largely symbolic when we come to ultimate things. It is but little that we know and that little changes. But instead of thinking of God as an enlarged human copy, enthroned somewhere eternally in the heavens, we need to think of God as pervasive energy, as ever present mind, inspiring the best. The world of intellectual abstractions, — abstract elements, abstract selves, abstract Gods, — is a barren world. The part must be fructified by union with other parts, above all by union with the best, the divine. For a God who has become an abstract idea, a name, we must substitute the consciousness of God as a living creative presence.

If God is energy, every reaction to God means a new creative synthesis in the universe. O, the infinite complexity of God's creativeness. Like light, God's presence breaks differently with the character of the prism; like chemical energy it gives rise to new properties, new individuals in the creative synthesis of our finite activities with His life. The total life situation counts in the creative presence of God, in the precipitation of our soul into His soul. God is incarnated, reborn differently under different conditions.

> "Life, like a dome of many coloured glass,
> Stains the white radiance of eternity."

It is not only in the matchless personality of Galilee that God is incarnated; but God is incarnated in a unique way wherever there is a new birth in goodness and beauty. Every true religious experience is a new creative synthesis. God does not repeat Himself in human relations any more than in sunsets or the play of shadows on the mountains. The external setting is the body of the occasion and cannot be divorced from the inner grace. God has all seasons for His own, His creative loyalty is the same, but His gifts differ with the occasion.

Most of the time we are so preoccupied with our practical tasks, with the cares of this world, that we are unmindful of the higher meaning of life. Habit and custom harden our minds to the finer moving of the spirit, the real poetry of life; and the glory of God cannot break through our inertia. In psychological language we say that these subtler influences and stirrings in us fail to rise above the threshold of our consciousness and so pass unperceived. But sometimes, — in days of love or sorrow or solitude or under the inspiration of a momentous occasion, — the threshold is lowered and the creative light of God streams in. We then perceive the persistent values of life, the deeper meaning and harmony to which we were blind before; and life is transformed for us, even as a great painting which at first seemed daubs of colour develops its perspective and wondrous values to the appreciative eye.

His presence comes to us in the calm and patient performance of the everyday tasks of life and brings us the satisfaction of work well done. It keeps us sane in the days of peace and smiling plenty; and it sustains our hope in the days of tribulation. It comes to us too in the sublime moments of life, whether in reverence for the majesty of the starry heavens above or the moral law within, and makes us triumph over our baser self.

Not only in tender moods of lovingkindness does it come, but in the stern moments of righteous wrath when innocence and virtue are trampled under foot. It is present not only in our passive moments of holy contemplation but in our strenuous moods too — in our sincere striving after truth, in our earnest fight against unrighteousness. Be sure that there comes a peculiar creative grace to those who work with sincerity for the good of the whole, for social improvement, who strive to excel in service for humanity — a grace which cannot come to the slacker and the idler. Wherever men work and fight in loyalty to worthy causes, His presence sanctifies and strengthens. Where the honest peasant tills his field; in the fisherman's lonely hut where the billows sob upon the shore; on the high seas where the seamen keep nightly vigil for their fatherland; on blood-stained battlefields where men fight in loyalty to a noble cause; to the patient toilers in the mines where the sun never penetrates; in the laboratories where men seek new truth; under the silent stars where true hearts pledge eternal troth; in the humble home where tiny baby fingers play the cords of love's perennial symphony; wherever men live in loyalty to the whole, there God's presence comes and blesses and makes life beautiful and holy.

God is especially present to those who give themselves for a great cause, vicariously and with a joyous heart. His presence makes sacrifice victory instead of tragedy. It makes the giving of life in a great cause a redeeming atonement instead of cruel murder. We do not think of the death of Jesus as murder, we think of it as atonement, for in his divine renunciation man and man, and God and man, were brought into nearer harmony. And God is present in the world's Gethsemane today, — stained crimson in the loyal sacrifice of youth in China, in Europe, in Africa, that freedom and justice and love may live and that a better humanity may blossom forth in the future. Wherever man fights for freedom, face to face with the naked realities of life; where man meets man untrammeled by conventions, free from the encrustations of false traditions, he learns to know the reality of God and man in the holy abandon to a common cause. A new tragedy is facing humanity. May it be a sacrifice for the healing of the nations in the consciousness of a common good. It has been said that "a good war hallows every cause"; but it must be *good,* and it can only be good when it is for a larger and better life. As we follow God into Gethsemane for the common good, so shall we follow him into the resurrection of a better humanity; and the golden star shall become the sign of the Prince of Peace.

God's presence always brings new meaning, new worth to life. It is different in spring, with its flowers and abounding hope, and in autumn, with its glory of dying nature; different in the rosy dawn of youth with its phantasy and its romance, from what it is at eventide when the shadows lengthen and the light mellows into the benediction of a life well spent; different through the mists of a mother's tear-filled eyes and in the gayety of childish laughter. But always it makes pure and holy and beautiful the moments of life when it enters. Always it brings hope and assurance of better things. It is a gladsome presence creating a joy that the world cannot give and cannot take away,

> "A peace above all earthly dignities,
> A still and quiet conscience."

The light of heaven breaks differently in different temperaments and moods — now with more gray in its harmony, now with more colour. Why should we think of the sombre temperaments and moods as being peculiarly religious? Why should the song of life always be a funeral dirge? Why not accept the gladsome moments and happy temperaments as godsent revelations of the goodness and brilliance of the higher life? Yes, and the moments of chaste humor too when God reveals the grotesqueness and incongruities of the life that is, and thus prepares us for saner living. "I am a part of all that I have met," says the poet. God can say: I am part of all that

admits me, all that is not shrunken by prejudice, hardened by
habit, or dead through sin — part of all that have ever realized
my presence in a new birth of insight. There He leaves, if not
His image, something of his creative energy and inspiration,
as the true teacher lives again in a new way in the souls of his
pupils.

He is infinitely sensitive to the moods and settings of nature
and suffuses them with unique beauty. He touches our souls
differently in the seasons.

> "These as thy change, Almighty Father! these
> Are but the varied God. The rolling year
> Is full of Thee."

The woods were God's first temples; and in their solemn stillness we may still feel the awesomeness in His presence that
our ancestors felt. We, like our ancestors for ages, feel a
peculiar inspiration in the high places, those friendly mountains that take us aloof from the humdrum of the world and
invite to contemplation, even as they invited Jesus to his
choicest moments with God. But there are the fields too with
their lilies and the song of birds, the prairies with their stretches
of waving corn and wheat, their delicate lights and shadows
and their homely variety, speaking of God's kindness and peace.
His presence soothes our weary hearts in the pattering rain.
He "overcomes us like a summer's cloud" with special wonder
in new discoveries of nature's laws. Even as of old to the
inspired poet, so now to the inspired soul: "The heavens de-
clare the glory of God; and the firmament showeth His handi-
work. Day unto day uttereth speech, and night unto night
showeth knowledge. There is no speech nor language where
their voice is not heard."

If the light of eternity is stained differently in the varying
conditions of nature, how much more in the varying contexts
of human history. God's creative presence reveals itself differently in different stages of development. It reacts differently,

shows different properties, in the infancy and youth of individuals and nations from what it shows in their maturity. As a
parent cannot be the same companion and friend to the child
that he or she can be to the grown-up son or daughter but
must share life in a varying way under the limitations and
characteristics of the different stages of development, so the
presence of God must take on different colour, different relations with the evolution of man. Every stage, when normal
and true, has its own unique beauty, its own divine significance,
but it is a different significance. And the relations which are
normal in an earlier stage are not germane in a later stage
and may even be immoral. The father must to some extent
be master and policeman to the immature child, but such a
role, if persisted in with a developed personality, makes moral
relations impossible. We cannot make a conception of God,
which was effective and normal in a primitive society, answer
the demands of a democratic people. And the same holds
inversely: We cannot make social standards which are the outgrowth of conscious moral relations fit a more primitive stage
whether in the individual or in the group.

Every epoch, therefore, in human development establishes
different relations with the divine. God is incarnated differently
in the life of the primitive Hebrews with their tribal organization, their heroic legends, from what He is in the age of the
great prophets with their national conception of justice and
order; differently in early Christianity with its glory of martyr-
dom, its intense expectancy of the dramatic end of evil, its
absorbing other-worldliness, from what He is in the later
Middle Ages with their organized ritual and sacraments and
their zealous domination of this world. In each case the revelation of God in human relations is effective and beautiful when
it is genuine, when it expresses God truly then and there.
What we must not forget is that conceptions and forms which
were real and vital in a past epoch of development may not

be relevant today. The new wine must have new bottles. God today seeks to incarnate Himself in twentieth century institutions, the dream of democracy, the hope of the masses, the liberty of man, woman and child, in international cooperation. And to resist the genuine movements for human betterment is to strive agaist God. One thing is certain. God's presence is always vital. It is never a mere tradition. It has to do with the creative expression of the best in the particular epoch in which men live. Past expressions become instruments to present living, but we cannot live in the past without making life unreal and thus being untrue to our own creative mission.

The divine presence takes on different colours, different creative values, according to the different genius of races and peoples. The ancient Hebrews were right that they were a chosen people. The world would be infinitely poorer without their lofty conception of God and their zeal for righteousness as preached by their prophets. It was meet and right that they should be loyal to their genius; and in so far as they were loyal to the inspiration of their prophets, they were indeed God's people; they had a mission altogether unique, — a light to lighten the gentiles in their moral strivings. Where the Hebrews showed the limitations of their age was in their blindness to the significance of the creative mission of other peoples. Such blindness may have had its place in human development in preserving the purity of the type and in intensifying loyalty to the meaning of life as revealed under specific conditions, even as mother-love's partiality to its own has its function in the economy of the whole. But such partiality is nevertheless a blindness; and in normal development, loyalty must broaden to insight into the beauty of other types of God's creative contribution.

God has revealed Himself not only in the moral austerity of the Hebrews, but in the sense of beauty and the love of reality by the Greeks. Who can estimate the contribution of the Greek mind in its art, its philosophy, its science? Who can deny that at their best they are an incarnation of the divine spirit of history? And we must recognize the divine creativeness in the genius of the Romans with their sense of order and law. It is also present in a unique way in the play of fancy of the Celts, with their art, their fairyland; for the fairy creations of noble imagination are God's creations and no one has gotten his full portion of life who has not sometime lived in fairyland. Yes, the joyous, delicate, exquisite moods of phantasy also belong to God, the inspirer of every pure and noble thought. So do the sturdy qualities of the Norsemen when tamed and hallowed in the chivalry of a holy cause, so does the passion for music in the Germans, so do the love for democracy and the homely virtues of the Anglo-Saxon. We are gradually awakening to the fact that the oriental peoples have made a unique contribution in art and story and that they have something magnificent to bring to the fund of humanity. We are beginning to see the beauty of the songs and harmonies of our once hunted precursors on this continent and also of a people that we but recently despised as slaves.

What we need to realize is that the soul of God seeks to incarnate itself in all these varieties of life and that their difference gives God his unique opportunity for creativeness. Human nature in any one mould or race is too limited to refract the whole beauty of God, to reveal all His properties. At best the revelation is fragmentary, but if we are tolerant and pure of heart, we shall learn to appreciate and reverence the unique contribution of God wherever it is made, and thus enrich our own fragmentariness with the larger mosaic of life. In every people, epoch or race, which strives to realize the best we may be sure of the creative grace of God. In God's infinite garden of flowers, there is a patch named America[1] and you

---

1 Insert your own nation.

are one of the flowers; in God's infinite mosaic there is a pattern named America and you are one of the colours; in God's infinite symphony there is a strain named America — our strivings, our hopes, our destiny — and you are a tone in that strain. Let us cultivate our garden spot; let us make beautiful our pattern in harmony with the whole as we can see it; let us make our strain the incarnation of the divine life in the world.

The consciousness of the creative presence must become pervasive in our life. It must include and sanctify all our human relations and all our relations to the universe. It has been customary to speak of the fatherhood of God, and this is indeed a significant relation. It was natural that, in the days of the patriarchal family, this relation should be singled out for especial emphasis. But the presence of God is incarnated in every noble and holy relation. The Hebrew prophets were right in conceiving God as the vital bond of their political life. They pictured Him as a husband and Israel as his rather fickle bride, and early Christianity represents the church as a bride decked out for her bridegroom. In the Madonna worship of the Mediaeval Church, God is conceived in terms of the highest feminine qualities, the tenderness of motherhood, and we too feel that the eternal womanly draws us onward. Motherhood, indeed, seems the fittest symbol of divine love. But the divine is incarnated in true filial relations as well as in parental, creating a divine reciprocal bond. It is manifested peculiarly in the relation of disinterested friendship: "I call you no longer servants but friends." It reveals itself in all true relations of brotherhood and kinship whether among individuals or groups. God incarnates himself in human loyalty at its best. When that loyalty is national, the best in human striving is national. But when human experience broadens, and the iron doors which close the hearts of nations open, then God will as surely

incarnate Himself in a still nobler way in the broader cooperation of nations. The consciousness of God enhances all true
communion with nature as well as man. It is the inspiration
of truth, righteousness and beauty the world over.

CHAPTER EIGHT

CULTIVATING THE PRESENCE OF GOD

Like love, like friendship, like appreciation of art, like true knowledge, like all devotion to the best, the presence of God must be cultivated. Indeed it is through such relations that we cultivate God. God is the best, and the best requires cultivation. There is truth, no doubt, in the saying of the poet:

" 'Tis heaven alone that is given away;
'Tis only God may be had for the asking."

The presence of God is not the monopoly of any caste or class. It knows no other apostolic succession than the communion of the faithful. It respects no artificial conditions of men. But it is not true that heaven comes to the idler and slothful. While it is a gift, it only comes to those who are prepared. It requires earnestness and wholeheartedness. Salvation must be sought with fear and trembling. Immortality is a prize which must be striven for with one's whole energy. The deeper flashes of insight come only in the stress and travail of the soul to attain better things.

It is true that there are times when you need to loaf and invite your soul. Leisure and play have their place. But they become fruitful only when they are the interstices of honest work for improvement. Newton may have discovered in a moment of relaxation the identity of the law of the falling apple and of stars falling in the vast expanse. But O! the work and patience which made the discovery possible and made it fruitful. "Badness, look you," says Hesiod, "you may choose easily in a heap: level is the path, and right near it dwells. But before Virtue the immortal gods have put the sweat of man's brow; and long and steep is the way to it, and rugged at the first."

Excellence in any field of endeavor requires denial and discipline. God does not love the slacker any better than we do. And sound, true men like what is hard. They are appealed to by sacrifice, if it leads to achievement. Loyalty is a deep motive in human nature, but it must be stimulated by a cause that is worth while. Youth is ready to die in the trenches, even though it resists the bribes of the church. It is a libel on human nature to offer it a lazy man's paradise; and a religion which does so is bound to fall into desuetude. If immortality were held out as a prize, instead of an idle privilege, the whole world would be fighting for it.

It has been customary to identify religious experience peculiarly with the neurotic type of mind and the harmonizing of its disorganized tendencies. In cases when there is a consciousness of a divided self and a long struggle of the worse against the better tendencies of human nature, religious unification sometimes comes by self-surrender. But this is after all merely the beginning of the religious life. The soul, like Jacob of old, must build an altar, it must fix the precious gift by some creative act of its own, to insure its possession. Emotion must become character to establish the title to ownership. If we identify God with the best, then it is plain that He cannot be had merely for the asking without earnest purpose and endeavor on our part. The best does not get itself accomplished by chance or dreaming merely.

> "Not from a vain or shallow thought
> His awful Jove young Phidias brought."

And even though the moment of inspiration may come as a gift, it is not likely to come unless the soul has previously been prepared by sincere and earnest effort. The kingdom of heaven comes to those who make violence upon it. The pearl of great price can be had only by sacrifice. God conceals the mysteries of life to all but those who are duly and truly prepared. The seed may be sown generally, the opportunity may be democratic, but only the best cultivated soil yields a hundredfold.

It is true that this cultivation must not be merely intellectual. A shallow intellectualism may indeed unfit one for the realization of the presence of God, as St. Paul and many others have felt. It must also be the cultivation of right emotions, a true openminded character, loyal human relations. But thought must be cultivated, too, for truth is of God. The whole moral life is summed up in the virtue of thoughtfulness. Our thinking makes a vast difference to our appreciation of the best, to our sensitiveness to God. We need creative imagination to grasp the beauty of the divine. The untutored fisherman can get something of value, but he cannot penetrate into the divine mysteries as can a St. Paul. It is not thinking, — real thinking — which is the enemy of the intuition of the divine. On the contrary, it is essential to the true sharing of the divine soul, to inspired creativeness whether in human relations or science or art. What kills our finer sense of values is the "cast of thought," crystallized habits and customs, which make us blind to new truth. Real, creative thought, creative imagination, is rooted in instinct and intuition. It feels its way into the future, like the birds their pathless way to the homeland, following its presentiments and testing them by the outcome. There is a poet in each one of us, if we can but coin our deepest souls into conscious and ordered expression. The deadness does not lie in thought, but in the inertia which substitutes counters for firsthand experiment, words for intuition. Thought and intuition are inseparable in sane living. Intuition without thought is like a man feeling his way in the dark. Thought without intuition, rooted in the realities of life, is a will o' the wisp, flitting about but accomplishing nothing.

It is a man's vocation to share the creative mind of God. The ancients were inspired by the consciousness of thinking God's thoughts after Him. It must ever be our striving to think God's thoughts, not only after Him, but with Him, for in all creative work we share the thought of God and help, in so far as we can, to bring it to pass. We must, however, be humble in our limitations. The child playing with Newton on the seashore gets something of Newton. It responds to his friendliness in its own trusting way. But the mind of Newton with its vision of universes is far beyond it. It can grasp it, if at all, only after long cultivation. We are only children walking hand in hand with God. But we must strive to share His mind by thoughtful meditation, for this is the door by which His creative mind can fructify ours. It is indeed a brave and a risky thing to think. But it is a riskier thing to live in slavish dependence upon other people's thoughts. For thus we miss the divine privilege of being a man. If we are sincere we shall learn by our mistakes, as the child learns to walk by falling. And inspiring us, guiding us through the ages, is the incarnate wisdom of God. We must, therefore, cultivate the divine gift of thought. And we not only must cultivate thought, but we must cultivate the sense of beauty, for God is the creative artist in the universe. He is the genius of harmony and order. The cultivation of beauty, therefore, makes us friendlier with God. We must cultivate our conscience, for God is the lover of right and justice. And in working for righteousness, we are working in God. We must cultivate love, for God is the sunshine and rain of mercy in the universe and the inspirer of all good deeds. Finally we must cultivate the spirit of communion with true men and God for in this spirit of fellowship, of abandon to a common cause, we become one with God.

All we know about the divine is that it is always the best, — the best of human thought, feeling and conduct, — and that it is the better still to be, the everlasting call to better things, — better art, better science, better personality, better society, better religion, better everything. And sin, evil, hell is being in love with the worse when the better is available. God's presence reveals itself in all those activities which tend toward sanity, harmony, and good will and away from mere impulse and chaos. He is the God of order and beauty, of right and of love. Whenever we strive for excellence, for the best, in order that we may enrich humanity with our best, and when we also encourage others to be and to do their best in the service of the whole, then we are in tune with God. Then we share the life in God, for God is the God of the best.

"He prayeth best that loveth best."

We worship God best when we do our best, when we follow the divine promptings to creativeness, to good deeds — not as artificial slavish acts, but as the blossoms and fruits of the spirit. When the soul becomes conscious of this creativeness in God, the giver of every good and perfect gift, then it has claimed its full inheritance. Then it recognizes itself as no longer mere man, but the incarnation of the God that liveth in it. "Finally, brethren, whatsoever things are true, whatsoever things are honest, whatsoever things are just, whatsoever things are pure, whatsoever things are lovely, whatsoever things are of good report, if there be any virtue, and if there be any praise, think on these things."

This is not saying that the individual single handed can realize the potentialities of man. There is a profound meaning in the doctrine which insists upon grace as an essential part of salvation, however onesided its emphasis has been. This does not mean that we need subscribe to the doctrine of the total depravity and impotence of human nature. Such a doctrine is a libel on man, and throws the entire blame upon God. The will of the individual must be taken into account as a determining factor in any ideal which makes life worth while. The appeal today must be as of old: "Son of man stand on thy feet." But while individual willingness is an ultimate ethical fact, we must not overlook the dependence of individual striving upon the larger life. The individual's efforts are futile except as they form part, though a creative part, of the matrix of social life. We are the debtors of all the noble souls whose efforts and sacrifices have made our opportunity possible, as well as of those who are working with us and shall work after us. Above us and through our fragmentary efforts, there is the creative life of God, reinforcing our best and giving unity to our ideals in the cosmos, in so far as they are worthy of survival. If in the economy of nature it is true that we arrange the conditions, while the creative energy of nature does the work, it is equally true in the realm of spiritual achievement that at best our willing and our efforts are but the conditions of the creative synthesis of our souls with one another and with the cosmic spiritual energy. It has been said that we learn to skate in summer and to swim in winter. Nature by its creative growth ekes out and perfects our efforts, though nature cannot accomplish the result without our efforts. So in the realm of creative spirit. The best thoughts and the highest coordinations of the soul come as gifts to those who earnestly will the higher life. How new flashes of insight come to us after years of seemingly fruitless efforts; how, after periods of discouraging failures, the higher coordinations of character all at once become easy is the miracle of all spiritual achievement, though if we had not tried patiently the gift would not have come. Thus creative grace makes real our will-to-the-good.

Think not yourself, or the world you live in, as mean and of no account. There is no human life so insignificant but that it may not become "a thing of beauty and a joy forever," if suffused and fructified by creative relations with God and fellowmen. Do not speak of yourself or others as common clay. There is nothing common in the universe when its full powers are realized. Charcoal and diamonds are made of the same material. The difference is in the process. The commonest soul in the stress of circumstance may show wonderful heroism and loyalty. There are infinite potentialities in you when compounded with divinity in true and sincere cooperative activities.

What stores of hidden energy may be released by the magic touch of a noble and passionate incentive. There is infinite loveliness in you when transformed by the alchemy of true human relations. The loveliness of the violet is not the loveliness of the rose. There is no common measure of beauty, but each has a unique loveliness. There is much goodness in you. You at your best contribute a loyalty which is to be found nowhere else, and the universe needs you to complete its harmony. There is much wisdom and sanity in you when you are sincere, when you read the universe in terms of your real experience — an insight which can be had nowhere else. It is true that you shine largely by borrowed light. Every soul must thus shine, and the greatest souls are those that borrow most. But each sincere soul contributes a new colour scheme, a new significance by its reaction, for each soul has a different texture. What is needed is that each soul shall find itself, shall discover its unique genius, shall strive for its best — to make God real in its own unique way.

Be creative as God is creative. Try to improve every task, however humble. Never be satisfied with what has already been accomplished. Do not lie down and betray your trust because you think your talent a meagre one. There is always the danger of the man, with but one talent, burying that. He has so little incentive. Make the most of what you have; and your powers of work and appreciation will increase a hundred fold. All work that is worth while is divine. God only knows what contribution is most significant in the economy of the whole. Certain it is that if you shirk your task, the universe is poorer, as it is richer by your creative effort. Opportunity always knocks at the door. Heed it early that you may have a long productive day in God's vineyard. But if it is the eleventh hour, still heed it. Perchance

"Some work of noble note may yet be done";

but something can always be done, if it be but an act of sincere

repentance and a manifestation of honesty of purpose. There
is no telling how much this may accomplish in the future in
your life and in the life of others. Do not work as a hired
man. Such a man never earns more than his hire. He misses
the main reward which is joy in one's work. Be a freeman,
make the work your own, give play to the creative impulse
within you. There is a divine restlessness which spurs us on so
long as we truly live. When it deserts us, we are already dead.
Be productive and be productive for the common good — that
is the eternal commandment. That is the joyous life, for there
is no happiness worth having except the consciousness of doing
something worth while. And the spring of living water, the
joy of doing for others, is always at hand. Such a life is a life
of comradeship with the divine Creator. It is a life of comradeship in sacrifice — giving oneself and forsaking all else —
but it is a joyous sacrifice. Such a life means humility, for the
best is always infinitely far ahead. Be loyal to the best and you
are loyal to God. Fortunate are you if it can be said of you:

> "Look, what is best that best I wish in thee;
> This wish I have; then ten times happy me."

Men have made God in their own image. And because they
have been stolid, stupid and unimaginative, they have conceived
God that way. But for His brilliance of imagination, His sympathetic touch, there is nothing commonplace. His creative
presence makes meaningful the infinite varieties of experience,
and even the humblest relations acquire infinite worth. To
the casual traveler the prairies seem monotonous. But there
is infinite variety in the prairies for the seeing eye — the blue
haze, the shifting lights and shadows, the varied colors, the
glorious sunsets, the purple afterglow of the day. There is
nothing common about life except ignorance and superficiality.
Each period, each age, has its own beauty in a life truly lived.
Life is like a tale that is told only to him who misses its
significance.

Such a consciousness of God's presence would revolutionize the prevailing conception of a static being, living apart from the world, who for a short time was present in Jesus of Nazareth and at intervals, mostly in the distant past and to the ancient Hebrews, sends a messenger from Himself. Rather must we think of God as ever present, ever creative, ever pervading the universe as our minds pervade our bodies, never working through delegated authority, operating throughout the cosmic process as the force working for order and beauty and righteousness, incarnated in the better instincts, the higher potentialities of life everywhere, no respecter of race or locality, manifesting Himself in the progressive historic mind, revealing Himself especially in the rarer creative moments of the human spirit and there producing new increments to our world — new insights, new values, a peace that passeth knowledge.

CHAPTER NINE

RELIGION AS SACRAMENTAL COMMUNION

It is a mistake to regard religion as a mere affair of the intellect. It is true that religion involves honest and thorough thinking, for truth is of God. A religion which does not keep thought alive becomes stationary, a victim of its auto-suggested superstitions. But true thought is rooted in social relations. It leads to communion. At best, thought is an uncertain though indispensable lantern. It must be sustained by the oil of faith. In the deepest relations of life, thought becomes symbolic of a reality which must be appreciated to be truly known. Religion is more than thought. It is a social bond, a spiritual compound in which the individual must enter into solution as salt in water in order to reveal his potencies. God is ever ready to enter into creative communion with those that are devoutly disposed. "The hour cometh and now is when true worshippers shall worship the Father in spirit and in truth: for the Father seeketh such to worship him."

Mediaeval religion was right that sacramental communion is a fundamental function of religion, but it became stereotyped and lost its power to minister to a growing life. The sacramental bond *is* the inmost life of religion, but it must be sacraments based on what is most true and vital in human nature — sacraments sanctifying real human relations and stimulating what is best in us, not a mere ritual based on a dead society. Since a sacrament is in its very nature a social institution, there must indeed be the outward and visible sign, but the true reality of the sacrament is revealed in the inward and spiritual grace which comes to those who devoutly share in a common faith and in a common activity for a great cause.

All vital human activities should be made sacramental as indeed they were in earlier religions. Mediaeval religion singled out those activities which seemed most fundamental to it and made them solemn and momentous. The initiation into the Christian community through baptism, and the celebration of the common bond of the faithful with each other and the Master in the Eucharist have always ranked as the basic Christian sacraments. The sacrament of confirmation came early to be a means whereby the responsibilities of the Christian community were impressed upon the plastic adolescent mind — a second initiation in order that the individual might share in the obligation which through infant baptism had become corporate. Penance, which emphasizes the continuous need of a right disposition, and confession, which keeps up the spiritual hygiene of the soul, were felt to be permanent needs and therefore treated as sacraments. Marriage needed to be solemnized by the consciousness of its being a divine as well as a human bond, in order to insure the constancy and holiness of the union. Induction into the monastic life and ordination to spiritual leadership in the church came naturally to be regarded as holy functions in the mediaeval conception of life. The extreme unction, the sacrament of death, emphasized the sublime faith of the church in the unity of the divine economy and gave the individual assurance for his last journey; and the sacrament of burial served alike to impress, under most solemn conditions, the transitoriness of life and the everlasting hope which is the very essence of Christianity. Historic Christianity has thus aimed to solemnize the social relations which have seemed to it momentous.

We need not less sacraments, but more than those of mediaeval religion, so they be based upon true and vital social relations. Life has changed in its emphasis and organization; and it has become vastly more complex than in the Middle Ages. Religion must strive again to cover all of life. It must emphasize the bond with the creative soul of goodness in all those relations that today are vital to human welfare. We need especially, in a democratic organization of society, a sacrament of citizenship. If mediaeval religion made a sacrament of the induction into its most characteristic institution, monasticism, so must we make sacramental the participation in a common life. We must make a religion of democracy, the most characteristic ideal of modern life. Only in creative partnership with God can we hope to make the brotherhood of man — of individuals and of nations — real.

On the intellectual side of life, there has always been and will always be diversity. Early Christianity had not one but hundreds of diverse interpretations. The church of the Middle Ages, the most submissive period in the history of thought, exercised a continuous discipline against heresies. When its theology was finally standardized, the old order was dead and the process of disintegration went on apace. Evidently a living religion must allow the largest freedom of experimentation on the intellectual side. This is the surest way for truth to be selected and to survive. But while the intellect is critical and unstable, emotional needs are largely constant. Hence sacraments have a permanency that creeds can never possess. They also have a universality that the intellect can rarely command. In some form, even if unconsciously, the divisions of Christendom pay tribute to the ancient sacraments of the church. There is in fact a greater unity of sacramental recognition than we ordinarily realize.

Baptism has practically universal recognition throughout Christendom, irrespective of denominational diversity in ritual and creeds. The Catholic church joins with nearly all the Protestant churches in recognizing all baptised Christians as members of the church universal. By a sound intuition, the only continuity that is here insisted upon is the continuity of the Christian community, and the only uniformity of ritual that is insisted upon is the simple baptismal formula of the early church. In this basic sacrament which, through the ages, has been the initiatory rite into the Christian community, there is at least an implied recognition of Christian unity which if fully understood should lead to new cooperation. The form of initiatory rite will necessarily vary with historic conditions. But there is always the consciousness of identification with the community. Of the spiritual continuity of the Christian community we can indeed be certain, while all theories of ecclesiastical continuity are at best speculative. We can also recognize a unity of Christian aim, however diverse may be the intellectual interpretations. The direction, in short, can be recognized as common in the midst of the accidents of historical development.

As regards the other great historic sacrament, the communion of the faithful, the celebration and revitalizing of the common bond, there has been less consistency, though even here the practice of open communion is becoming nearly universal among Protestant denominations. It is manifestly inconsistent to shut out from the Lord's Supper, which is the great community sacrament, those who are recognized as members of the church universal. It would seem that if any sacrament is to be recognized as universal, it should be the communion of the faithful. It should be the privilege of all who are devoutly disposed, in love and charity with their neighbor and who intend to lead a new life. The Lord's supper is the oldest of all the Christian sacraments, for it was instituted by Jesus before His death. It did not originally presuppose even baptism, since baptism as a Christian rite did not originate until some time after the death of Jesus. It certainly did not for a considerable time presuppose confirmation, since the sacrament of confirmation can hardly be said to exist in New Testament times. The text cited for it in the book of Acts is ambiguous and seems to have to do with a peculiar theory of receiving the Holy Ghost, analogous to the revival idea of "having religion." That the fitness for corporate communion rests with the individual and not on any objective evidence of receiving the Holy Ghost is evidenced by the fact that Judas Iscariot was not barred from the first communion table.

The frank recognition of the Lord's Supper as the corporate communion of all professed followers of the Nazarene would go farther towards unifying Christianity than any rigid intellectual agreement which, in the nature of things, is impossible. The sincere recognition of the common bond could not help leading to important practical results of cooperation and would nullify the appearance of schisms to those outside. If we already recognize that diversity of ritual and creeds does not invalidate the sacrament of initiation into the Christian community, why should such diversity prevent the celebration of the common bond by those who recognize one another as Christians? If the validity of initiation rests on the continuity of the Christian community, the sacrament of communion is the very essence of that continuity.

The sacrament of confirmation is a beautiful and appropriate adolescent rite, but is naturally associated with membership in the particular denomination. The other traditional sacraments have suffered transformation and lost much of their significance outside the Catholic church. It is a pity, I think, that the sacrament of confession has fallen into disuse. It has great therapeutic value. And we suffer for a lack of a sacrament of democratic citizenship. Any true and vital human relation can become a sacrament when God is made a part of it. What we need is that the deeper sacramental consciousness — the consciousness of the creative participation of God in all true and loyal community bonds — shall be made a fact in our modern life and permeate our social relations.

It is not desirable that we should sacrifice local or institutional associations in the ministration of sacraments. We do not want dead uniformity in sacramental ritual any more than in intellectual interpretation. The symbolic aspect of each sacrament has its nucleus in early Christian practice and can be enriched, as it is, by each denomination to meet its particular needs. Each body of Christians has its traditions which enrich its life and which are means of grace to those living in them. Nor need we be afraid to borrow from mediaeval liturgy, which has a beauty and spiritual depth never attained at any other time. We do not require modernism in sacramental ritual whatever may be our requirements as regards creeds. What is desirable is that identity of purpose shall be recognized and that the authority shall be seen to lie, not in the peculiar features of ritual or theory, but in the continuity of the Christian community. It is earnestly to be hoped that we shall at least realize, in times of normal relations, the catholicity and tolerance that, by grace of God, have characterized the spiritual ministrations of the battlefield. We shall awaken some day to the fact that we need, and God needs, the significant differences as well as the unity of purpose. Sacramental harmony is not only consistent with, but enriched by, the difference in timbre of the different instruments. There can be no doubt that greater Christian grace shall come to those who thus live in love and charity with their neighbor.

In the rapid integration of humanity into ever larger unities there is not only the danger that religion may fail to keep pace with the movement, but there is another danger, not less real, namely, that religion may neglect the ancient loyalties in its zeal for the larger unities. Primitive religion was local. Its gods were household gods and community gods. The religion of nationalism, both in ancient and modern times, has tended to efface the local sacraments. In our changing, delocalized society, we have largely lost the family sacraments and the community sacraments. Yet can there be any doubt that the family and community are poorer and less stable because of the loss? God is just as truly the God of the family and the God of the community, as He is God of the nation or of the universe. We need to restore the sacred intimacies of the primitive sacramental religion, enriched by the greater perspective of life that we possess. Instead of ecclesiastical divisions, we need the consciousness of the community of one holy purpose. We need a religion which shall stimulate the community to realize the best life; and we need a religious damnation of the slacker, the parasite and the profiteer.

Now as of yore the soul must have its shrines, its sacred places. It is a poor soul that is not rooted in the soil, that has not some holy of holies where love's incense rises, some Bethel where earth and heaven meet in holy communion. Is God partial to places? Certain it is that He depends upon the total life situation for his creativeness. And the place made hallow by traditions, by symbols and architecture, embodying the creative genius and devotion of a community, is the body of its collective spirit, even as the individual soul requires a physical body. This soul of a sacred place, of a vital institution, has its continuity, its development, its cumulative mind, which grows richer with the years; which becomes conscious in collective ideals by which men are swayed and for which they are ready to sacrifice. Happy the soul that has such a Mecca to which it can look back in loyalty and to which it can make pilgrimages. It is not the sacred places that need to be demolished but the blindness which would prevent our bringing the richness of our local shrine into the common fund of life.

We may be sure that wherever there is the marriage of true souls in a holy purpose, there God is present in creative fruitfulness. And it is not indifferent to God what the shrine of the soul is. The presence of God as it comes in the old cathedral, with its stained glass windows and gothic arches, with its venerable traditions and sacraments, is different but not more real than as it comes to devout worshipers where two or three are gathered together in His name in the humblest meeting house. The beauty of holiness is more important than the beauty of setting, though the setting should express the genius and devotion of the soul.

There are indeed times when the soul needs to retire into itself in communion with God. In these silent moments God's creative presence does hover over the soul, fruitful as Jupiter's shower of gold, overshadowing it like the Holy Ghost the Virgin Mary. When we turn from hypocrisy and arrogant commonplace enthroned in high places, then we may assert our independence in the words of Emerson:

> "For what are they all in their vain conceit
> When man in the bush with God may meet."

But it must not be forgotten that God is a social God and that He is present with his creative grace whenever men meet in sacramental devotion and there creates a new bond. He is present wherever men cooperate earnestly with the whole abandon of their souls in a great human cause, guiding and making sane and fruitful their counsels and endeavors. For He is a God that works in human relations. Wherever kind, pure, and wholesome bonds are created, there he adds the divine ingredient which sublimates their loyalty and makes them nobler than they are. It is through social relations that our insight and inspiration in the main must come. And it is the fruit of such relations which makes solitude significant.

In this communion of the faithful, there can be no real distinction between the quick and the dead. "The communion of saints" is an article of the creed which, however neglected in this mechanical age, has profound and permanent significance. Here the sensitive soul of a poet like Maeterlinck may be more trustworthy than the scepticism of the superficial agnostic: "The souls of all our brethren are ever hovering about us, craving for a caress, and only waiting for the signal. But how many beings there are who all their life long have not dared to make such a signal! It is the disaster of our entire existence that we live thus away from our soul, and stand in such dread of its slightest movement. Did we but allow it to smile frankly in its silence and its radiance, we should be already living an eternal life." We may not be able to prove to the sceptic the reality of our communion with those who have passed beyond the curtain, but neither could we prove to such a mind the reality of the communion with the souls on the hither side. Love and friendship cannot be demonstrated to the senses, real though they are to the eye of faith and momentous in their consequences to those who live them. And the true souls, who live in the presence of the unseen, shall have the evidence — not in the disordered and commonplace ravings of some modern Sibyl, so much as in the sympathy of a common love and the incentive of a common faith.

Millions of the world's youth "have gone West" in the great world tragedy. Shall they not count? Shall not their sacrificial loyalty be a leaven of redeeming love to bring humanity, friend and foe, together into a common bond of understanding and sympathy? Yes, and are they not with us even now, stimulating our better feelings, urging us forward to greater sacrifice, to more heroic endeavor, to greater self-forgetfulness in the common cause? Are not West and East but different exposures of the same life, even as sunrise and sunset are but the same great light of day from different perspectives? Are not the quick and the dead bound into one fellowship in the great life of the universe; and is it not the grossness of our intellectual perception which makes us fail to realize their common push with us toward all that is best, even while we are moved forward by it, — combining their energies with ours, as the myriad silent impulses of the sea combine into the mighty wave?

It was a tragic thing when the abstract intellect put heaven and God far away in space. It meant that man lost his sense of living relations with them unless under exceptional conditions; and those came to seem more and more unlikely with the progress of science. Hell somehow has always seemed nearer and the devil more active. When God sowed the good seed and went away, the devil was busy and sowed tares. What we need to realize is that heaven and hell are here about us and in us. Heaven is all that which is constructive, which binds together into larger unity, which makes for concord, harmony, and beauty, whether in the seen world or the unseen world about us. Hell is all that is destructive, which makes for strife, and discord and ugliness in this world and the unseen world. The seen and the unseen world, little though our coarse powers of perception realize it, are one — one communion of saints or one hell.

PART THREE

LOVE AND INSIGHT

CHAPTER TEN

THE TWO POINTS OF VIEW

In the prologue of the drama of Job, there are presented two interpretations of life. There is the point of view of Satan who has traveled much and observed much. He has no lack of facts. Like Goethe's Mephistopheles, he can say: "I am not omniscient but I know much." But the facts are all seen in the philistine perspective of selfishness and cynicism. To him Job does not worship God for naught. He is certain that if the favors are withdrawn, Job's loyalty will end. On the other hand, we have the point of view of God, the lover of men, who has faith in his servant Job in spite of his frailties and limitations. He looks at Job through the eyes of sympathetic appreciation, not through the eyes of cynical criticism. He sees the potentialities of Job's life and measures Job in terms of the ideal for which he strives rather than in terms of actual attainment. The two points of view of the drama are typical of human interpretation. Which is the truer point of view? Which reveals the real nature of things?

The philistines have always boasted of superior insight and have always treated the idealistic point of view with scorn. They imagine themselves to be disinterested observers; and they suppose that it is the other point of view which is prejudiced. They emphasize the sordid and mean facts as the typical facts, and they call this realism. They regard ideals as a mere chiaroscuro, mere subjective embellishments of our world, having nothing to do with reality. Their world is a collection of things held together by external bonds. There is no inner unity. The point of view of love, on the other hand, emphasizes the inner unities and harmonies. It is the appreciation of a whole in which the fragments find their meaning. Ideals are of the very constitution of things. They are the warp which integrates the threads of life into a unitary pattern. Both points of view are keys with which men try to unlock the secrets of the universe. The question is which works.

The point of view emphasized in this chapter is that love alone furnishes real insight. The ancients painted love blind, but the wise Shakespeare gives us a deeper interpretation:

"Love looks not with the eyes, but with the mind;
And therefore is winged Cupid painted blind."

It is not love that is blind. It is the rest of the world that is blind. The colour blind can see the world only in drab grey. If most people were colour blind they would no doubt insist that the perception of colour is a mere illusion on the part of the rest. But in reality the world is a world of colour and beauty. Just so love adds a new perspective, a creative insight into the meaning of things, —

"The light that never was on sea or land;
The consecration and the poet's dream."

It is a mistake to assume that truth is something that can be perceived by the mere intellect and that the rest of our nature must be ruled out. There is, in fact, no "dry light." Our whole nature, emotional and volitional as well as intellectual, enters into our interpretation. Our patterns of ideas are simply the index of this reaction of our total personality. Thus it is that the jaded wretch can see nothing in the world but his empty cynical self. The wholesome, kindly personality can see good in everything — except sin. In each case, the universe is coloured by personal reaction. The question is: which colour harmonizes with the universe? To this there may be no answer in the abstract, but the human heart is confident that the point of view which looks toward development, which is constructive of greater harmony, which is conducive to more life is the key which unlocks the meaning of the universe.

I am choosing the name, love, rather than the thinner name of loyalty, because loyalty is but a paler reflection of love. Love has its roots deep in human nature. It is this elemental emotion, especially when it shines forth on the higher levels of evolution, which sheds a new effulgence over the world. Animals cannot be said to love because they cannot idealize. With them the sexual impulse seeks its satisfaction, and when the impulse is satisfied, the attraction is passed. They do not apprehend potentialities, ideals, the common bond. The crude instinct of animal life must be sublimated first into parental love and then into the larger love which gives insight into all things, human and divine.

Love knows the soul of things, not the mere surface. Hence it can see beauty where the uninitiated see only the commonplace. To the lover new secrets, new traits, new merits are ever unfolded. How understanding people are when they love some one! How much they see which escapes the rest of the world! Nothing is mean or commonplace.

No more striking example of the two points of view could be furnished than that in Tolstoy's novel, *Anna Karénina*. Levin and Kitty have at length found their common love. How transformed is Levin's entire world. In the evening he attends, in company with his brother, a local council with its routine of small business and its long debates. He had had little sympathy with such efforts at local government. But this night he sees it all in a different light. "Levin listened all the while, feeling that the money to be expended, the sewer pipes and the rest, were of no serious importance; they were only a pretext to bring together pleasant, congenial people. Nobody was bored, and Levin noticed with surprise — from some trifling incidents which once would have entirely escaped his notice — that he could now penetrate the thoughts of each of the speakers, read their souls, and see what excellent natures they possessed; and he felt that they all liked him. Those who did not know him seemed to speak to him, to look at him pleasantly and in a friendly manner. 'Well how do you like it?' asked Sergei Ivanovitch. 'Very much; I never should have believed it would be so interesting.' " Even the watchman at the hotel becomes an object of interest and sympathy. "Never before had he paid any attention to him; but he suddenly became aware that he was a good intelligent man, and, above all, kind-hearted." All barriers are leveled and he succeeds in overcoming the restraint of the watchman and in entering into his life, — to discover that he has a family which he loves and for which he has ambitions.

For the other view of life, we have the revelation of Anna at the close of her tragic career. She has tasted the stolen sweets of life and they have turned bitter. Love has turned into hate. Without realizing what she is doing, she is hurrying on the train to the scene of her tragedy. Everything seems mean, ugly and empty. She looks with disgust at the deformed woman passing below the car window who is "followed by a little girl laughing affectedly." A husband and wife who seat themselves opposite her in the compartment and who try to be sociable are obnoxious to her. "Anna clearly saw how they bored each other, how they hated each other. It was impossible not to hate such painful monstrosities. The second gong sounded and was followed by the rumble of baggage, noise, shouts, laughter. Anna saw clearly that there was nothing to rejoice at, that this laughter roused her indignation, and she longed to stop her ears. At last the third signal was given, the train was going to start, the locomotive whistled, and the gentleman crossed himself. 'It would be interesting to ask him

what he meant by that,' thought Anna, looking at him angrily."
She looks into peoples' hearts and sees nothing but deception.
At last a chance suggestion flashes on her disordered mind:
"Why not extinguish the light when it shines on things dis-
gusting to see? But how? Why does the conductor keep hurrying through the car? Why does he shout? Why are there people
in this car? Why do they speak? What are they laughing at?
It is all false, all a lie, all deception, all vanity and vexation."
And the unconscious logic of such a life of unreality and
emptiness drives her to the fatal end. She throws herself in
front of the locomotive. What did she see in the retrospect
of death? "And the candle by which she read, as in a book,
the fulfilment of her life's work, of its deception, its grief,
and its torment, flared up with greater brightness than she
had ever known, revealing to her all that before was in darkness, then flickered, grew faint, and went out forever."

Which is the truer view? We must judge philosophies as
trees—by their fruits. Levin's awakened love opens up a
broader and more sympathetic life. The glow of the first days
cannot always be maintained, but as emotion settles into sentiment and habit, it fits him for the larger companionship with
men, it makes him a builder of institutions and a link in the
larger development of the race. Anna's valuation of life leads
to anarchy, misery, and death. Each philosophy verifies itself
in terms of the experience of the individual. But considered
from the point of view of humanity, present and future, one is
livable, and the other is not. If philosophy is the guide of life,
the philosophy which is livable is the true philosophy.

In another of Tolstoy's great novels, *War and Peace,* the
hero, Pierre, who is visiting the battle scene is unexpectedly
taken prisoner and for some time is obliged to share all the
hardships of his fellow prisoners. It was then that a new light
came into his life as he learned to associate with human beings
under the simplest conditions of democracy. New heavens were

opened to him through the simple christian love of his humble, dirty and ignorant fellow prisoner, Karatieff. He learned that the uncouth peasants were real human beings and found much to love and to admire in their simple patience and ruggedness. It was then, in short, that the beauty of the simple life in true human relations came to him, and that, in spite of the sordid conditions of the prison camp, he learned the beauty of nature and of human nature. At night "Pierre cast his eyes upon the firmament, filled at that hour with myriads of stars. 'All that is mine,' he thought. 'All that is in me, is me! And that is what they think they have taken prisoner! That is what they have shut up in a cabin!' So he smiled, and turned in to sleep among his comrades."

It is this same revelation of life which Maeterlinck, in a more mystical way, strives to convey in the *Blue Bird*. Mytyl and Tyltyl in their children's dream of fairyland have had a great adventure in following the mystical Blue Bird. When they wake up, it is evident that their heart has been touched with a new emotion. The humble home looks fresh and attractive to them as it never has before. The little sick neighbor girl for the first time looks beautiful. Yes, she does look like the fairy of light who was their guide in dreamland. In their childish kindness they give up their own bluebird in the cage to the sick girl who had long desired it; and then they discover that the bluebird at home is like the bluebird of their dreams, perhaps not quite so blue, but he will be bluer. In the light of childish love, the humble and previously commonplace surroundings have been transformed into a happy harmonious paradise. The good, but commonplace parents cannot understand the children, but it is clear that the dramatist feels that they have brought back for a moment the real meaning of life.

Everywhere the contrast is the same. In the days of George Washington there were the sceptics who said that the Union was an idle dream. They had nothing but criticism and fault finding for Washington and his supporters, and were ready to betray him at every turn. There were on the other hand the simple folks who felt the goodness and wisdom of Washington; who loved him and believed in him and were willing to make the last sacrifice for the ideal of democracy. It was so in the days of Abraham Lincoln. There were the critics who saw nothing but failure, who maligned him in the most scurrilous manner, striving to impugn his motives, to sow distrust and disunion. But there were on the other hand those who loved Lincoln, who felt the integrity of his motives, the sanity of his insight, and were willing to make the utmost sacrifice in order that his insight and his love of the common bond might be realized.

It was even so in Palestine in the days when Jesus walked upon the earth. There were the critics, the people blinded by their own prejudices and their own selfishness. Even his nearest friends were found quarreling over places of prominence in the new Kingdom. Thousands of sick sought free healing and forgot their benefactor. Thousands followed because of the loaves and fishes. At length the envious and blind rulers who saw nothing in him but a disturber of the peace and a rival for power, brought him to the cross. On the other hand, there were those who in their own simple way genuinely loved him, and through their love, saw a great light. Their lives were ennobled, their spirit of sacrifice was stirred; to them came, in the course of time, the Pentecost of a great faith. Renan tells us that Christianity is built on the hallucination of an hysterical woman. Rather it was love that saw what the blindness of the world and the fear of the faint hearted could not see — the new hope beyond the tomb, a living Saviour.

Then there is the point of view of Jesus himself, so difficult for us to understand because we are so far from the quality of his life. The world of Jesus lies suffused in the golden light of love. It shines with the light of God. And it is through his love of God and man that he possesses his wonderful insight. It reveals both the better and the worse part of human nature — the infinite potentialities and the hypocrisy. It is a democratic light which shines on all men alike, irrespective of station and previous condition. It shows that good may be found everywhere and where we least look for it. He can see good where others see nothing but evil — in publicans and prostitutes. He can see infinite beauty where others see nothing but commonplace. He can see good in the fisherfolk of Galilee, as well as in aristocrats like Nicodemus and Joseph of Aramathia. To him the potentialities of the humblest are infinite. He recognizes an ingredient of divinity everywhere, even in the repentant thief on the cross. He has the genuine philosophy of democracy, because he *lives* democracy. For him there is nothing worthless that God has made. His ideal is that of service for all; and he is greatest that serves best. But the final consummation is friendship: "I call you no longer servants but friends." For friendship is love's choicest blossom and fruition.

Yet if the love of Jesus brings into relief the potentialities and beauty of life, it also brings into relief its baseness. No one as he has scourged insincerity, hypocrisy, malice and selfishness, in high places. His denunciations of the Scribes and Pharisees would be brutal did they not come from the heart that loves all things both great and small, and hates only their perversions.

Humanity has rightly felt that in the life of Jesus we are looking at the world through the eyes of God, as far as our finite limitation permits. God is love, for God is the constructive, healing, unifying spirit of the universe. Love of God is but the yearning for perfection, the larger meaning of life, harmony and health of soul. Love is of God because the true soul has an instinct for improvement, for better things. It sees beyond the superficialities, beyond the chaos; and divines the constructive principle which works for righteousness, order and beauty; and in that insight becomes itself a creative factor in bringing harmony out of chaos. Since man's instinct for idealization cannot be satisfied in human relations, the human soul seeks a completer object of satisfaction, a deeper bond. This bond is not an abstract unity but a mind which can react, which can give and respond, which through its infinite goodness ennobles all other bonds and gives the soul those relations it most deeply craves. God is the light that suffuses the universe with meaning and value.

CHAPTER ELEVEN

LOVE AS INSIGHT INTO GOD AND THE UNIVERSE

It became the fashion in the Middle Ages to try to establish the existence of God from the abstract concept of being. Having defined God as the most real being, the mediaeval theologians tried to deduce the existence of God from the definition. It has often been pointed out that this is a mere circle and establishes nothing. We get out of definitions what we put into them. But what about the definitions themselves? What validity have they? If we start, on the other hand, from the sentiment of love, we shall get a surer clue to the existence and nature of God. It is the best of sayings that God is love. If God is love we must grasp God through love. Love is always of goodness, of perfection. Love demands the existence of a perfect object, — the reality of its ideal striving. Whence otherwise our sense of incompleteness and imperfection? Whence this divine restlessness and dissatisfaction unknown to the animal world? Whence come these "intimations," these "broken fragments of light," this longing and striving for the perfect, if there is no basis for it in the universe?

These ideal demands cannot be fulfilled in the world that we actually find. The world in its totality cannot satisfy them. It is not an object of love, for it is the mixture of good and bad. It contains much that is incompatible with what we love and for which we strive. Hence love's eternal demand that there must be a being in the universe that satisfies its craving for perfection, for goodness and beauty in personal relations. The existence of such a being may not be capable of exact proof; but love is ever ready to risk its all upon its faith in such a reality; and it is in that faith, and that faith only, that

love succeeds in bringing to fruition the highest potentialities
of human nature. It is only in this bond with the unseen and
greater good that love can realize the maximum of goodness in
the finite bonds — those personal and group relations which
constitute our immediate vocation. Only thus can love reach
the highest ideal in human loyalties. The demand for a perfect
object of love must have as much reality as the finite and in-
complete efforts to which it leads. In some way the universe
must recognize and reciprocate the yearning and striving for
perfection which it prompts in its parts. The realization of the
good life is possible only in a universe which furnishes the
possibility of the highest personal relations. A merely automatic
enforcement and registration of the past, a merely impersonal
moral constitution, will not suffice. There must be the beckon-
ing of the future, the stimulation, from a greater love, of our
best — an energy flowing into our life and working for goodness and beauty, re-enforcing the better angel of our nature.
In this consciousness lies the life and inspiration of ideals. This
infinite good-will gives strength to organization. It furnishes an
inexhaustible basis of friendly cooperation. It must live, for
only in its kindly and encouraging atmosphere can anything
else live that is worth while — in fact can anything continue
to live, for life means unity and cooperation.

If theology had tried to derive God's existence and qualities
from love instead of the abstract concept of self-existence, its
results would not have been so utterly barren. Love is the mediator between our feeble finite insight and the ideal which we
seek. The whole essence of God is expressed in the character-
ization, "God is love," if we can but see the implications. You
can derive God's *constancy* from His love. Love is loyal through
all the changes and chances of life.

> "Love is not love
> Which alters when it alteration finds,
> Or bends with the remover to remove;

O, no! it is an ever-fixed mark,
That looks on tempests and is never shaken;
It is the star to every wandering bark,
Whose worth is unknown, although his height be taken.
Love's not Time's fool, though rosy lips and cheeks
Within his bending sickle's compass come;
Love alters not with his brief hours and weeks,
But bears it out even to the edge of doom."

Through all the limitations of life, through all our failures, we feel that the eternal love abides. Perhaps the nearest we get to it is in mother-love. The world can see nothing in the condemned criminal but ugliness and badness. The mother still sees an object of affection. She still finds something good in him. Think, how the world must appear to God when suffused with the light of His affection. Nothing hopeless, nothing damned, that redemptive love cannot awaken into new life, if but the willingness is there.

Love is of justice. Justice, righteous indignation, has its roots in the parental instinct, whence it spreads to the protection of the innocent and defenseless and to the wronged everywhere. Love is a consuming fire against selfishness and oppression. It punishes the transgression against love. He that does not love his brother, but treats him as a mere thing, shall indeed bear the mark of Cain. He shall lack real happiness, real peace of soul. He has made himself an outcast by cutting himself off from the bond of human beings and the universe. Love means fair play. It means the right of every man to the opportunity to realize the best that is in him. True love, love sublimated and enlightened by an ideal, is always just, but it is more than abstract justice. It is constructive justice. It makes men just. It is the creative encouragement of all that is best in us, of all attempts to harmony and health in the soul of the individual, in society, and in the universe.

Love is wondrous wise. It is God's sympathetic sharing of our life which makes God understand us and we Him. Love reveals, as it inspires, the true values of life. In its golden light are seen not only things as they are, but things as they can be and ought to be. It is a creative insight through which we know more than we know and can do more than we do, because it seizes on the future and reveals the larger implications of life. And it not only reveals but makes them come to pass. How much we can do in the warm and tender light of encouragement; how we are stimulated by the common love and the common faith. It is not what we are, but what we can be which is love's concern.

Love means power. It is not an abstract concept, but an energy which warms and inspires all that is best within us. Nothing is impossible for it which is worth while. The only things impossible are degradation and destruction. It works for ever-new harmonies; for ever-greater and nobler bonds; for a fairer and better world. And since love means growth, development, health, greater life, greater harmony, we can see that love in the end is all-powerful, because nothing can persist which is not in harmony with the whole. Love is loyalty to the spirit of improvement and progress — not rejecting the old, because it is old, but always ready to abandon any ways of thought and action, however time-honored and whatever may be the cost, when they conflict with our better insight.

Love is always genuine; it demands sincerity and wholeheartedness. It hates sham and hypocrisy.

> "O, how much more doth beauty beauteous seem
> By that sweet ornament which truth doth give!
> The rose looks fair, but fairer we it deem
> For that sweet odour which doth in it live.
> The canker-blooms have full as deep a dye
> As the perfumed tincture of the roses,
> Hang on such thorns, and play as wantonly
> When summer's breath their masked buds discloses;
> But, for their virtue only is their show,
> They live unwoo'd and unrespected fade;

> Die to themselves. Sweet roses do not so;
> Of their sweet deaths are sweetest odours made.

Unity is not only a characteristic, it is the very essence of love. Love is a cohesive force, it binds the parts together into a whole. But the unity of love is not an abstract unity. It is realized in concrete variety and individuality. There is no conflict between variety and unity in the bond of love, as there is in men's abstract philosophy. Love is a reciprocal bond where the whole is enriched by the encouragement and realization of the parts; and the parts find their vocation and joy in the life of the whole. In the true family bond, each member is made richer for the love of all, and each contributes a unique share to the unity of the whole. We all feel infinitely poorer for the loss of any member, even the least. It is so in friendship. The common bond enriches us and makes us more than we otherwise could be. Our best powers are stimulated. Each brings and finds fresh wonders of significance. The bond is not a third abstract fact as between two friends, but is a unity including them, living in them, and they in it. And so in the highest relations with the unseen — the divine moments of worship. It is not God and man and a mediator added, but God in man and man in God — an enveloping bond, stimulating "all holy desires, all just counsels and all good deeds."

Love means peace and harmony of man with man and of group with group everywhere. Not peace at any price. Redeeming love, love of progress, seems to bring not peace but the sword. Man to be true to love must be willing to sacrifice all for love.

> "Though love repine, and reason chafe,
> There came a voice without reply, —
> 'Tis man's perdition to be safe,
> When for the truth he ought to die."

Yet though love must carry on its eternal warfare against oppression, injustice and all that divides man from man, its aim is not strife but greater harmony, greater cooperation of man with man, and of people with people, greater happiness in loving the best and in working for the best everywhere.

Love is always of beauty. Even when love leads to abstract science, it is still motived by the love of harmony. Physical beauty is but the sign of the inner harmony which shines through and organizes the world of sense. Love proceeds therefore instinctively from the outer to the inner beauty which gives the outer meaning. "So that if a virtuous soul have but a little comeliness, he will be content to love and tend him, and will search out and bring to the birth thoughts which may improve the young, until his beloved is compelled to contemplate and see the beauty of institutions and laws, and understand that all is of one kindred, and that personal beauty is only a trifle; and after laws and institutions he will lead him on to the sciences, that he may see their beauty, being not like a servant in love with the beauty of one youth or man or institution, himself a slave, mean and calculating, but looking at the abundance of beauty and drawing towards the sea of beauty, and creating and beholding many fair and noble thoughts and notions in boundless love of wisdom; until at length he grows and waxes strong, and at last a vision is revealed to him of a single science, which is the science of beauty everywhere." It was such beauty that inspired the divine Plato. Men who really love truth are compelled first of all by the beauty of truth, the unlocking of the hidden harmonies and their mathematical simplicity. The practical use comes later. In our deeper personal relations, it is still the love of beauty that actuates us — the love of the potentialities, the striving for the ideal, the love of the beautiful soul which shines through every mien, gesture and act, the love of the inner harmony with man and God. And the love of God is of the eternal realization of beauty, of perfect harmony of life, the harmony which draws us to itself and inspires in us the love of beauty and perfection.

Love not only reveals the meaning and beauty of human nature, its tragedies and comedies, but it also reveals the wonder and beauty of nature — beauty such as was never seen before and as the materialist's eye can never see. It enables the soul to enter into a new communion with the soul of nature, it overcomes the deadness of our habits and of our intellectual abstractions. "Love all God's creation, the whole and every grain of sand in it. Love every leaf, every ray of God's light. Love the animals, love the plants, love everything. If you love everything, you will perceive the divine mystery in things. Once you perceive it, you will begin to comprehend it better every day. And you will come at last to love the whole with an all-embracing love." So speaks Father Zossima in Fyodor Dostoevsky's novel, *The Brothers Karamazov.* Without the tender light of love there can be no appreciation of beauty. The pessimist looks at the starry heavens and sighs: "Heck! it is a sorry sight." The prosy soul looks and sees so many "gnats." The materialist in his deadness sees only dead mechanism. The profound moralist looks and is inspired with unspeakable awe and reverence. The lover of nature and man looks at nature and feels the inner harmony of soul with the universe which the others cannot appreciate, because they have not the necessary sense for its perception. Nature discloses her secrets only to the lovers of nature. She does not speak to the churl or the egoist. She admits the matter of fact man only into the vestibule of her temple, not into the inner sanctuary. She chooses for her high priests sincere spirits and lovers of men — noble souls filled with divine enthusiasm for truth. To them indeed she reveals her laws and uniformities, but she does more: she reveals her very soul.

It is not only that "true knowledge leads to love," but rather true love leads to knowledge. Only to the noble and disinterested is the deeper truth of things vouchsafed. Contrast the lover of nature, the man of poetic imagination, with the drudge, the mere collector of facts. The latter is like Peter Bell:

> "A primrose by a river's brim
> A yellow primrose was to him,
> And it was nothing more."

His prosy, mechanical soul remains untouched by the beauty about him.

> "The soft blue sky did never melt
> Into his heart; he never felt
> The witchery of the soft blue sky!"

Much less could he feel that deeper community which made nature to Wordsworth a living reality, full of soul and meaning:

> "To every natural form, rock, fruit, or flower,
> Even the loose stones that cover the highway,
> I gave a moral life: I saw them feel
> Or linked them to some feeling: the great mass
> Lay bedded in some quickening soul and all
> That I beheld respired with inward meaning."

Only when we recognize that nature is the loving art of God do we appreciate its true significance. This does not mean pantheism. We must not confuse the artist and his material. There is much in nature that is unformed and maladapted. But the lover of nature sees the beauty, too. The reason that love is the key to nature is that love is a striving for harmony, unity, and simplicity. And it is this tendency in the universe which makes it possible to know. It is because eternal Love works for beauty, right, and harmony alike in the larger cosmos and in human nature that the true lover feels at home in the universe. He is in rapport with the force that works for beauty. He sees through the chaos of detail, the trappings, into the creative soul of things. He has constructive faith in the ultimate harmony of the soul within and the soul without. Unless indeed the outer order as well as the inner is ruled by harmony and beauty, our appreciation and striving is futile and meaningless.

Call not this a mere subjective valuation, a mere pathetic

fallacy. It is the wooden materialist, the man blind to the deeper harmonies of nature, the man without music in his soul, who is subjective in his deadness and conceit. For him a stone is a mere stone, a tree is a mere tree. For him a house is a heap of bricks. He fails to see the constructive unity, without which science and beauty are alike impossible; and he prides himself on his stupidity. Such a man can do little to advance the cause of truth. He is a slave of routine. He cannot rise to the consciousness of a Newton — the consciousness of being in his Father's house. The great scientific geniuses have been poets.

Science, as a mere abstract technique, a mathematical calculation of probabilities, misses at best the individuality, the uniqueness of nature everywhere — all that constitutes reality in the full sense. It deals with abstractions, averages. It furnishes certain skeleton keys with which we can unlock kinds of facts. But it unlocks more than it reveals. It needs to be supplemented by the individual appreciation of art and religion, with their intuition of the living unity which works for order and harmony in our world. Poetry has its place as well as the convenient abstractions of science. Science, divorced from life, is without soul and may become an instrument of heartless destruction. A true view of nature must make us appreciate nature as well as dissect her. It should produce that tenderness that prevents unnecessary suffering and destruction; that establishes companionship with the birds and flowers — not the maudlin sentimentalism that lavishes care and affection on animals while it neglects human beings, but a love which sees the presence of God, and admires His beauty and loveliness everywhere. The constructive energy of the universe made us for this end and made nature for this end that these unique harmonies should be revealed to those that are prepared to appreciate them — to the real lovers of nature. To discover the meaning of nature we must have poetic intuition, imagination touched with emotion; we must be enamored by its beauty.

There is no neutral light. The philistine is not really neutral, but distorts everything with his conceit. Rather let us dream with the poet and be taught by love the inner harmony of things:

"How sweet the moonlight sleeps upon this bank!
Here we will sit, and let the sounds of music
Creep in our ears: soft stillness and the night
Become the touches of sweet harmony.
Sit, Jessica, look how the floor of heaven
Is thick inlaid with patines of bright gold:
There's not the smallest orb which thou behold'st
But in his motion like an angel sings,
Still quiring to the young-eyed cherubims;
Such harmony is in immortal souls;
But whilst this muddy vesture of decay
Doth grossly close it in, we cannot hear it."

Love is of immortality. It is love of infinite development, of infinite creativeness. For love, time and eternity are not contradictory but complementary. There must ever be movement, richer development, more significant novelty, new surprises of beauty and meaning. Yet, in the variety of change, there is the unity of direction, the persistence of the ideal, realized in every new content and getting its colouring from it, — the continuity of form in the midst of the ever-shifting material. Only thus can a whole be realized. A static world would leave no room for creativeness; it would be the frustration of the very nature of love; it would mean ennui and death. On the other hand, a world of mere flux, of infinite detail would mean utter weariness and hopelessness. The ideal of love, therefore, is the immortality, not of substance, but of development. It is the unity of direction rather than the unity of statuesque completeness.

Love ever demands that what it deems of worth shall survive. It strives to bring to fruition the infinite potentialities, the larger meaning of all that is individual. Its demand for infinite creativeness can only be realized in an infinite process.

In its grasp of the ideal, it makes circumstance its raw material; it rises superior to alteration, and seizes upon the eternal beauty of the fleeting moment. Love, as Plato points out, is not only love of the good but of the eternal possession of the good. This eternal possession of the good can be had only in a world of infinite development. Thus time with its ceaseless flux must be interpenetrated with the eternity of form; and form must be incarnated in the flux of time. Only thus can love go on. For the love of immortality is the demand for the eternal going on and development of love.

This love for immortality shows itself, however unconsciously, in the love of racial continuity. The promise of the group, the salvation of the race can be realized only by the on-going of life. Israel must persist if the promise to Abraham is to be a reality. Humanity must go on in ever new editions, life taking up the torch of life, if the greater humanity, the greater hope, which makes the striving and sacrifice of each generation worth while, is to be a reality.

In a more spiritual way, love shows its craving for immortality in ideal creativeness. Love strives ever to realize itself in those unities of poetry, art, science and institutions which conserve the net results of the spiritual victories of the past and make possible greater creativeness for the future. Without this ideal continuity, — the tradition embodying the results of past creativeness and making cumulative significance possible, — mere racial continuity would not be worth while. This ideal continuity is the conservation of the soul of the race and its development, as biological continuity is the conservation of the blood of the race and its cumulative adaptation. Love therefore must ever strive to re-create itself, in soul as well as in body.

Finally, there is the demand of love that individual worth shall be indestructible, that personal relations shall be conserved. Love demands that love shall go on in those choice concrete relations which constitute, in the last analysis, the reality of love.

> "Oh never star
> Was lost here but it rose afar."

This does not mean an individuality crystalized into a statue, like Lot's wife. But the love of an individuality of creativeness, of new development, of new meaning. Such an immortality implies risk. It is not to be had for the asking, but is a prize to be gained, a laurel wreath worthy of man's noblest efforts.

"If by any means I might attain unto the resurrection of the dead. Not as though I had already attained either were already perfect: but I follow after, if that I may apprehend that for which also I am apprehended of Christ Jesus."

CHAPTER TWELVE

LOVE'S CIRCLES

Love begins and ends in personal relations. All else is but instrument. Love of human beings begins in one and spreads, in normal life, into the family affections, into community love, into public spirit, into patriotism, into love for humanity. "And the true order of going or being led by another to the things of love," says Plato, "is to use the beauties of earth, as steps along which he mounts upward for the sake of that other beauty, going from one to two, and from two to all fair forms, and from fair forms to fair actions, and from fair actions to fair notions, until from fair notions he arrives at the notion of absolute beauty and at last knows what the essence of beauty is." Love thus proceeds from the nearer to the more remote, from the outward to the inward beauty, from the personal to the superpersonal. This same idea is emphasized by Emerson in the platonic spirit: "In the procession of the soul from within outward, it enlarges its circles ever, like the pebble thrown into the pond, or the light proceeding from an orb. The rays of the soul alight, first on things nearest, on every utensil and toy, on nurses and domestics, on the house and yard and passengers, on the circle of household acquaintance, on politics and geography and history. But by the necessity of our constitution, things are ever grouping themselves according to higher or more interior laws. Neighborhood, size, numbers, habits, persons, lose by degrees their power over us. Cause and effect, real affinities, the longing for harmony between the soul and the circumstance, the high progressive, idealizing instinct, these predominate later, and ever the step backward from the higher to the lower relations is impossible. Thus even love,

which is the deification of persons, must become more impersonal every day."

But however love spreads into the larger and more abstract
circles of experience, it must ever remain rooted in the concrete
and personal; and it must find its culmination in the personal.
The larger, more comprehensive loyalties must be fed by the
instincts that give rise to the more intensive ones. The former
are the foliage and crown of the latter. The love of truth
must have its basis in concrete immediate facts. Else we lose
ourselves in barren speculation. The love of beauty must be
in the first instance and all the time the love of concrete beautiful things, however much it may be necessary to analyze them
and reconstruct them in order to bring out their full significance. The love of goodness and virtue must be first of all
and always the love of goodness in the concrete — concrete
acts, real personal relations. When the love of virtue becomes
merely abstract and institutional, it loses its real significance
and fails to affect and illuminate actual human life. Institutions
are but instruments in the realization of personal goodness and
must not be allowed to become ends in themselves as they are
too prone to be. As soon as an institution is definitely under
way, and especially when it becomes large and powerful, it is
the tendency of human beings to regard it as the chief thing
and the people as mere instruments. They fall down and
worship the idol of their own making.

Love must reveal itself first of all in human personal relations. We must see some particular human being in the light
that flares up from the elemental passion of the human heart
and discloses, if but for a moment, the infinite riches of another
human soul. The beloved soul is all that and infinitely more,
could but the light of love be kept burning. This has been
beautifully expressed, even if perhaps with somewhat too
pagan exuberance in Walt Whitman's poem "To You":

"Whoever you are, now I place my hand upon you that you be my poem;

I whisper with my lips, close to your ear.

I have loved many men and women and men, but I love none better than you.

O I have been dilatory and dumb;

I should have made my way to you long ago;

I should have blabbed nothing but you, I should have chanted nothing but you.

I will leave all and come and make the hymns of you;

None have understood you, but I understand you;

None have done justice to you — you have not done justice to yourself;

None but have found you imperfect — I only find no imperfection in you.

O I could sing such glories and grandeurs about you;

You have not known what you are — you have slumbered on yourself all your life;

What you have done returns already in mockeries.

But the mockeries are not you;

Underneath them and within them, I see you lurk;

I pursue you where none else has pursued you.

Silence, the desk, the flippant expression, the night, the accustomed routine, if these conceal you from others, or from yourself, they do not conceal you from me;

The shaved face, the unsteady eye, the impure complexion, if these balk others, they do not balk me;

The pert apparel, the deformed attitude, drunkenness, greed, premature death, all these are put aside.

There is no endowment in man or woman that is not tallied in you;

There is no virtue, no beauty, in man or woman, but as good is in you;

No pluck or endurance in others, but as good is in you;

No pleasure waiting for others, but an equal pleasure waits for you.

Whoever you are! Claim your own at any hazard!

These shows of the East and West are tame, compared with you;

These immense meadows — these interminable rivers — you are immense and interminable as they;

You are he or she who is master or mistress over them,

Master or mistress in your own right over Nature, elements, pain, passion, dissolution.

The hopples fall from your ankles — you find an unfailing sufficiency:
Old or young, male or female, rude, low, rejected by the rest, whatever
  you are promulges itself;
Through birth, life, death, burial, the means are provided, nothing is
  scanted;
Through angers, losses, ambition, ignorance, ennui, what you are picks
  its way."

There is a revelation of divinity in a unique way wherever
there is genuine friendship and loyalty. Christianity has been
right in emphasizing the unique divinity of Jesus. There is no
measuring rod by which we can measure divinity. But Jesus,
as no one else, satisfies the human heart as the incarnation and
exemplar of the eternal Love. The world cannot love and
honor Jesus too much, — if it does so in his spirit. But to
recognize and love the divinity of Jesus does not mean to deny
or to belittle the potential divinity of other human beings whom
he taught to pray "Our Father," and whom he recognized as
children of the same God. Intolerance is not the result of the
gospel of the Nazarene, but the contradiction of it. We must
remember, too, that we cannot express adequately the beauty
and meaning of any individual life in any formula. How, then,
can we hope to express the life of Jesus in that way? We must
love the divinity of Jesus, the spirit of Jesus, in order to understand it. It has been obscured by an antiquated theology, expressed in terms which are unintelligible to most people today.
It must reveal itself first of all in emotion and conduct, in a
life genuinely lived. Each age must express the life of Jesus
or any other significant life in terms of its own concepts, but
realizing that all such expressions are provisional. The danger
is not that we love and appreciate one personality too much.
To the loving soul, there are indeed infinite resources, infinite
things to admire in even the humblest individual. The danger
is that we may be blind to the significance of other personalities.
We do not love one human being less because that love also

appreciates the significance of others. Rather is our love then more sane and valuable.

As in personal relations, so in group relations. Here, too, love must spread. We do not love our own family less because we love other families nor do we love our own nation less because we learn to love other nations. Rather do we enrich the love of our own family and of our own nation. It is true that we cannot love another family just as we love our own. There is indeed a certain reality for us in the more immediate relation which the more remote circles of life cannot possess. This implies a certain blindness which seems inevitable in human nature and indispensable to human effectiveness. No reorganization of humanity can be successful which fails to take account of these human limitations. Human nature is constituted first of all for face-to-face relations. It is from the smaller circles of intimate firsthand relations that the larger more remote circles must get their significance. Nor is there any prospect of changing human nature radically in this respect. The reality of our human relations is conditioned not merely upon our instincts, but upon our memory and imagination. No more people can be real to us in a firsthand sense than we can treasure in our memory and represent vividly in our imagination. Our instinctive love is necessarily limited by these factors which are practically permanent. The larger organizations are largely impersonal and therefore instrumental to the more personal relations. It is from personal relations that we must get the incentive to right living. If then the more intimate circles of love and interest are deleted, the larger circles will necessarily become confused and lose reality. This makes the importance of loyalty to family and to neighborhood. This is what gives the small national unit the advantage for spiritual purposes over the large centralized political powers. We must save, therefore, the ancient loyalties. We cannot spread our love impartially over all of humanity without making it too thin to be effective. But we can cooperate for the large human ends.

God, we may believe, loves comprehensively. To Him, therefore, the total perspective of life is ever present, and each part has its unique place in His affections as in His vision. And the love of no part encroaches on the claims of another. If we could love as God, we should see, as God, the significance and value of every man and group, each in its own temporal setting. Yet even though this is humanly impossible, we can and must to a certain extent break through our centrism and strive to comprehend the larger unities of life. This can be done by cultivating a larger thoughtfulness as to the meaning of human relations and a more comprehensive religious insight into the worth of man. He does not love his own nation less who can see the beauty of other nations — their ideals, their striving, their sacrifice, their loyalty. We are not less national now because we have come to love other nations, and are willing to sacrifice for them. On the contrary, we are saner now and have a more real appreciation of the dignity and worth of our own nation than we had before. It is the nature of love to overflow and to spread into space and time in all directions, even as light radiates. It is in these broader human relations that we learn to approximate and to appreciate the love of God.

No more striking illustration can be had of the effect of our emotions upon our insight than is found in the history of group relations. In the days when the clan was the unit of human appreciation and loyalty, there was incessant war between clan and clan. One clan could see no good in other clans. In the course of time, clans found it necessary to combine under pressure of common circumstances and common needs. They came to recognize a larger kinship. Neighborhood of interest begot friendly relations. The blindness of fear and mistrust gave way to understanding. They formed a new bond of sympathy and cooperation. It has always been thus. Friendship creates new understanding. Two old nations, the English and the Scotch, who for centuries carried on continuous warfare, with mutual hatred and mistrust, have been reciprocally enriched by the common bond and in unity have built one of the great civilizations of modern times. While England and France were carrying on continuous hostilities for centuries, they could see nothing good in each other. Each nation belittled the other nation's attainments. Voltaire referred to Shakespeare as a barbarian. A long tradition of misunderstanding and vituperation made it well nigh impossible for a man of either nation to see through the dark glass of his national prejudices anything but demerit and selfishness. What a marvellous transformation there has been in the understanding by these peoples of each other since they entered into friendly relations with each other.

Hate, on the other hand, blinds a people to the significance and reality of other peoples. This is as true in international relations as it is in personal relations. This accounts for the gross miscalculations which imperialistic Germany made, in spite of her vaunted science. Blinded by her national ambition, she failed to understand the reality of the bond which bound the British commonwealths to their mother country. She failed to understand the bond of friendship between France and England and the potential unity, not only of the English speaking nations, but of the democratic nations of the world — a bond of common ideals. Throughout Germany's international dealings in the last generation and the calculations preceding the great catastrophe, it has been Germany's blindness in an emotional way which has accounted for her stupidity in an intellectual way, in spite of all her genius for organization.

It is true that for the time being hate may solidify the national bond. But it cannot have the endurance of good will. It is a dangerous enthusiasm at best, — a yielding to the blind instinct of the herd to destroy indiscriminately whatever is in its path. When it breaks against superior moral resistance, it is followed by an equally unreasonable fear and panic. If hate and a fanatical nationalism could have held a nation together, it should have held imperial Germany together, where hatred of competing nations had been systematically cultivated by the ruling class. But it was because Germany went to pieces morally in the first world war that she finally collapsed in a military way. A nation with the resources of Germany but built upon justice and humanity could never have been defeated. Justice and good will are a stronger and more durable bond than greed and hate.

If there is to be a true and enduring peace among nations, there must be an organization on the basis of friendship instead of the armed balance of mutual jealousies. Nations must rise to the consciousness of moral personalities. They must learn to recognize one another's claims. They must come to see their interdependence in realizing all those things that are worth while — higher moral development, the discovery of truth, the creation of beauty. They must awaken to the fact that humanity is the supreme thing; that humanity outside the national fences is as significant as that inside, and that a national ideal which means the impoverishment and destruction of those outside is immoral and is bound to fail. We must get rid of the illusions of false pride of race and the insane obsession of power. Instead of dissipating our energies in armed camps and devices of destruction, we must turn science and organization into channels of mutual cooperation. In the end, a social regime which leads to sane cooperation and mutual understanding will prove the strongest bond of defense, for love and sanity will ever prove more coherent and more durable than hate and blindness.

Love creates bonds of unity and therefore furnishes the only insight by which such unities can be understood. This is as true of group relations as of personal relations. The unsocial group, like the unsocial individual, fails to enter into such bonds and therefore can see only the fragments — bricks without mortar.

Such an individual or group lives as an almoner or criminal in the midst of society and its institutions. Only he who loves his family, his community, his country, understands the bond which binds them together. Love understands because it is the architect. Love is constructive insight. It not merely quickens the perception for beauty and significance in human relations, but it helps to create and conserve those very relations. Hence love is rightly the first, the great and only commandment.

Out of the instinct of love, sublimated into purposeful striving, there grows all the deeper insight into life — into its harmony and unity, but also into its baseness. For only love can know and estimate truly the mean and detestable. The neutral and insipid cannot really know the bad any more than the good. They are the same to them. A person or a people who remains indifferent to outrages to women and children, to wanton and brutal destruction of all that is choicest in civilization, is not one who loves, but one who is incapable of love. It has been said by an ancient philosopher: "By love do we see love, and by hate, grievous hate." This is only half true. We do not see hate by hate. Hate and selfishness cannot see their own ugliness and deformity. It is only by love that we can see the enormity of hate and brutality. It is only love which can feel the discord of "sweet bells jangled out of tune and harsh," and the keenness of this sense of discord is one of the powerful motives for its removal. The ear which lacks the sense of harmony is not pained by discord.

"Love your enemies." This is the hardest test. But as a great lover of men, William James, said, if no one were "willing to drown his private wrongs in pity for the wronger's person, the world would be an infinitely worse place to live in than it is now." We must be willing to take the first step. If each party involved in a conflict, whether personal or group conflict, sits back in pharisaical pride and waits for the other party to repent, the misunderstanding will go on and accumulate. It is less important to place the blame than to establish good will. We must ever condemn whatever endangers the welfare of humanity. We must strive to protect the innocent and to enforce justice whether the criminals be individuals or groups. Sometimes a whole nation runs amuck and reverts to the primitive. Yet we must have in mind the potentialities; we must not only leave open the way for good will, but we must show good will, if we would have peace. And we must not be too self-righteous in judging the conduct of other nations. No nation can go back very far into its history without finding a skeleton in the closet. We must look to the future and do all in our power to create a fairer world. Love is always of the good; there must be something good in a people which has the coherence and loyalty to sacrifice to the utmost even in an unworthy cause. This loyalty must be redeemed for the cause of humanity.

Hate stimulates and perpetuates hate. We cannot win a victory worth while by hate. The motive must be love for humanity. For such a love we must be willing to sacrifice. Through this love, we shall gain new insight into human relations. We shall thus lay permanent foundations for good will and peace. We must love not our own nation less but humanity more. We cannot love blindness, perversion and bestiality. We can only love that which is truly human. But it is our duty to do our utmost that true humanity may come to light and realize itself in ourselves and in others. Our loyalty must ever be enlightened by our love for the good. Not will to power, but will to goodness must be our motto. In this spirit, our striving, whether in war or in peace, shall be sanctified for a permanent cause.

It is hard, if not impossible, to see sanely in the passion of a great war. It is part of the instinct of self-preservation that we should feel strongly about our own and that we should be blinded to the other side. It gives one comfort to think that in the past, in spite of the animosities of bitter wars, the healing love of humanity has asserted itself and that in time, sometimes in an astonishingly short time, new bonds have been created. We are at the crossroads of history. Great historic tendencies are clashing for supremacy. In these great moments, individuals seem to count for little. We are actors within a great destiny, the whither of which we can but dimly see. But we must work and sacrifice in faith for ideals as we see them. We must be loyal to our highest insight to the end, confident that the cause of a larger and freer humanity shall eventually win. In the meantime, may we, at least in retrospect, have the grace to see our enemies as the poet martyr, Sorley, in lines addressed to Germany shortly before he gave his life:

> "You are blind like us. Your hurt no man designed,
> And no man claimed the conquest of your land.
> But gropers both through fields of thought confined
> We stumble and we do not understand.
> You only saw your future bigly planned,
> And we, the tapering paths of our own mind,
> And in each other's dearest ways we stand,
> And hiss and hate. And the blind fight the blind.
> When it is peace, then we may view again
> With new-won eyes each others' truer form
> And wonder. Grown more loving-kind and warm
> We'll grasp firm hands and laugh at the old pain
> When it is peace. But until peace the storm,
> The darkness and the thunder and the rain."

The most gigantic tragedy in human history ended in a sordid peace, and a war which was fought to end war has begotten another and even more terrible war. It has become the custom to sneer at the idealism which actuated millions of men and women to sacrifice for a better world and to forget the cost of the selfish nationalism which brought on such a tragedy. But if we forget the lesson of this tragedy we shall make for greater misery in the future. The song of Flanders reverberates as a warning and a menace:

"If ye break faith with us who die
We shall not sleep
Though poppies bloom in Flanders fields."

It depends upon our faith, courage and good will whether the blood shed so recently and in such a flood, and is now being shed, shall be for the healing of the nations or a cry for vengeance.

It is our earnest desire and prayer that, out of the great crisis through which humanity is passing, there may emerge a larger bond of human beings, a larger insight into human relations. But such a bond can be created only by a genuine love of humanity and a willingness to help and to encourage all that is true in human nature. It cannot be a bond of suppression and hate nor a bond of the selfish interests of those involved. This would prove now, as it has proved in the past, to be a mere rope of sand and must crumble when the passion is over. An effort has been made to start an organization of nations to administer justice and to preserve peace; and such a consummation is devoutly to be wished. But no league can have any permanency or be binding upon those concerned, unless it is based upon a genuine sentiment of loyalty and helpfulness on the part of the groups and individuals involved. No constitution, whether national or international, can be more than a scrap of paper if it does not express the spirit of justice and of good will of those concerned. International machinery is valuable only as it is the genuine instrument of an enlightened conscience and a sound character on the part of the nations participating. Fear may hold a nation in check for a while, but at most it only awaits the occasion to strike back. We must all learn the significance of sacrifice for a common cause, if we are to entertain the hope of a stable society.

This aspiration for a unity of humanity does not mean the

.ubolition of such unities as have proven of genuine value to
the realization of human ideals. We have not abrogated the
family because we have found it necessary to establish the
larger unity of the community. Nor can we afford to sacrifice
the value of local loyalty in the greater bond of the nation.
The smaller unities must ever give reality to the larger ones.
In the community of nations, which must be the next step in
human organization, each nation must regard as sacred its own
heritage, it must ever strive to realize its own unique mission,
as this grows out of its past and is defined through its own
particular history and character. But this mission must ever be
consistent with the unique moral realization of other nations.
The ideal must ever be, not merely to live and to let live, but
to live and to help live. No nation liveth unto itself or dieth
unto itself. It is part of the larger life and realization of
humanity; and its life is significant precisely in so far as it
ministers to this larger end. A nation which so lives cannot die,
shall not perish, even though the accidents and blindness of
circumstance may for the time being deprive it of its political
existence. It shall ever be a leaven in the life of the race; and
if it is true to its best, if it is capable of forming an articulate
part of the larger life of a free race, it shall in the ages reassert
its individuality and win the immortality which it deserves. This
larger ideal of humanity is not consistent with a narrow centrism, an intolerant insistence by each nation upon its own
claims. It implies, on the contrary, a moral recognition of the
worth of other nations and a cheerful willingness to further
that worth. Not "Deutschland ueber Alles" any more than the
cleavage of Hebrew and Gentile, Greek and Barbarian; but
humanity above all, the realization of the potentialities of
human nature in the unity of a common bond, — not Pan-
germany nor Panslavism nor Pananglicanism but Panhumanity.

The world may settle the problem of the relation between
nation and nation. We may be able to demonstrate the futility

of overweaning pride and lust for power. We may be able to
restrain and curb recalcitrant nations by an organized public
sentiment, backed by adequate police power. We may look back
upon international wars as complacently as we now look back
upon the feudal fights of generations ago. But is the problem
settled then? Does this mean peace? There remains the perennial problem between man and man, the problem of human
opportunity, — the problem of the have's and the have-not's,
the problem of the fallen and outcast, the whole problem of the
personal association of human beings. This problem cannot be
settled merely by scientific organization. Science does not make
people less selfish and unscrupulous in personal, any more than
in group relations. Nor can it be solved by the restoring of
old sanctions, — the resurrecting of old beliefs or institutions.
It can be solved only by sympathetic personal insight, by the
recognition of the moral claims of every man, woman and child.
We shall have peace on earth only when the commandment,
Love your neighbor as yourself, becomes instinct and character
with human beings, instead of an intellectual formula, —
words hypocritically preached but never taken seriously in
conduct. We must learn to see humanity as Jesus saw it, — in
the light of love. We must recognize human beings as the
children of God, as members of one divine family, — falling,
erring children perhaps, but yet children of infinite potentialities. The increase of human opportunities and human worth
must become the aim, rather than the amassing of riches and
power. We must have the love that overflows, as the love of
Jesus overflowed, that can pray even for the malefactors.

It will take a long time to change the selfish and predatory
instincts of human beings. It means the development of a new
type of man, where love and fair play are the dominant characteristics. Unless we can develop this instinct to live for one
another and to sacrifice for one another, — not only for
present humanity, but for future humanity, in order that love

may go on and the race develop — the outlook is indeed dark. Science becomes an instrument of destruction placed in the hands of irresponsible madmen. It is not likely that we shall abandon the illusions of the past without further discipline in the school of bitter experience. We must walk the path of pain until we learn that love and helpfulness are the secret of living. May our path be thorny, may the floods of disaster rise to meet us, may the skies be brazen both in our personal and group relations until we learn to conquer the will-to-power and learn to inaugurate the will-to-the-good, a will guided by sane thoughtfulness and inspired by a high idealism as to the value and dignity of man. But if love and helpfulness once become the predominant passion, then we shall indeed see human beings as good fellows. Then friendship shall be the crown of life. Then we shall see God and good everywhere; and our loyalty to the divine shall create a new heaven and a new earth. Then the rivalry shall be to encourage and realize the best in ourselves and others. Then man shall find joy in his work.

> "And only the Master shall praise us
> And only the Master shall blame.
> And no one shall work for money
> And no one shall work for fame.
> But each for the joy of the working
> And each in his separate star
> Shall draw the thing as he sees it
> For the God of things as they are."

And for the God of things as they ought to be.

Love is the root of religion. Whatever you love with all your heart and with all your soul and with all your mind, that is your God. It may not be the God that you profess, the God that you have read about in a book. Here lies the hypocrisy in our religion: people profess one thing and love another thing in their hearts, never considering that it is the latter that is their religion — the religion that shapes their lives and by which they unwittingly pass judgment upon themselves. If their heart is set upon pleasure or upon power or upon wealth, regardless of others, making others a means to their selfish end, that is their religion — or their blasphemy because it is a denial of their true selves and therefore of true religion. If human beings could only be unmasked, if they could only see themselves as they really are, if the light could penetrate into their cave of illusion, we should have a revolution in human conduct. But they would more likely ostracize, or even put to death, if their power extended that far, the one who should reveal their nakedness. They get great emotional comfort out of worshiping idols — phrases, forms that have lost their substance and no longer disturb their selfish conduct. They make a God out of property and turn a deaf ear to the cry of human beings in need, forgetting that they brought nothing into the world and shall bring nothing out of the world except the ghosts of their soulless selves.

True religion is the sincere love of humanity. "Inasmuch as ye have done it unto one of the least of these my brethren, ye have done it unto me." It is significant that those who are placed on the right hand, those who are saved, in Jesus' great parable of the Final Judgment, had not been conscious of being religious. They had done all in their power to be helpful to human beings, expecting no other reward than the love they had shown. According to the theology in which they had been brought up, they never thought of their human love as having anything to do with God. But they are saved, not by the pronouncement of the great Judge — He merely affirms their salvation as a fact — but because they live "in love and charity with their neighbor." They are attuned to the great universal Love which through the ages works for healing and harmony in our world. We may call this Love by human names or we may not name It at all. But we worship It, though we know it not, when we share in the universal Love. Divinity may be expressed for us in one human being who calls forth our unqualified devotion, as did Jesus to his followers, but it spreads to other human beings as far as our love can reach. Because of Jesus' intense feeling against the inhumanity, perpetrated under the cover of religion, he places the conventionally religious, the hypocrites, on the left hand of the Judge, as the damned. There are no doubt others also who are damned by their selfishness but he ignores these. The theology of the saved and of the damned was the same, namely, that religion has nothing to do with human relations. But the damned — and that is the reason that they are damned — failed to show love in human relations. Their religion consisted in lip-service and ceremonies to a God throned afar — a God who does not exist and therefore could not save them.

Love is the light of the world. It is the key which unlocks the universe. Love is the key to human relations. It reveals the golden images within the exterior of clay. It opens up the true inwardness of man to man and of group to group. It binds them in a common bond of appreciation and sacrifice. Love is the key to nature. It makes us see beyond the routine into the inner harmony and art of nature. Love is the key to the invisible. By it we enter into communion with an invisible God and the good men and true of all time. Love is the mediator between our fragmentary selves and the more perfect whole of the future. Love is the fulfilment of the law. Without it our virtues are but an empty show, "clanging brass and tinkling symbal." Out of love springs constructive faith which makes us share in a common cause; and love paints the future in the colours of hope. Where love is dead, faith and hope must die for want of sustenance. In the great trinity of faith, hope and love, "the greatest of these is love," for it is the parent, the life-blood of the other two. Thus the eternal goodness and beauty which for the materialist are not, because he is dead to them, himself a slave of routine, mean and calculating, are made a living reality to love and become the perennial inspiration of the best.

PART FOUR

CREATIVE DESTINY

CHAPTER THIRTEEN

INDIVIDUAL DESTINY

"We live in succession, in division, in parts, in particles. Meantime, within man is the soul of the whole; the wise silence; the universal beauty, to which every part and particle is equally related; the eternal One." Our present life is but a moment of a larger whole. It is a plant whose roots stretch back into an indefinite past and whose tendrils stretch forward into an indefinite future. This human nature of ours, with its instincts and intimations, has been long in the making. It is fraught with a meaning larger than we can grasp. We live in succession and our little moment of consciousness that we call our life is curtained off backward and forward. The past history of the soul is wrapped in mystery. We cannot follow it beyond the curtain of this little existence. It may be that Wordsworth is right in his poetic conjecture:

> "Our birth is but a sleep and a forgetting:
> The soul that rises with us, our life's star,
> Hath had elsewhere its setting,
> And cometh from afar.
> Not in entire forgetfulness,
> And not in utter nakedness,
> But trailing clouds of glory do we come
> From God who is our home;
> Heaven lies about us in our infancy.
> At length the man perceives it die away,
> And fade into the light of common day."

But we cannot know; and the heaven which lies about us in our infancy is the hopes and aspirations of the race, only to be realized in an indefinite future. We are part of a destiny which we cannot see and can only dimly feel. Certain it is that life is more than the present. It is part of a larger whole which is somehow prospectively immanent in us as the direction of life. In this sense, the kingdom of heaven is within us, could we but realize its meaning. Destiny lies within us as the very law of our nature. Destiny lies about us as society striving to guide our stumbling feet in the dim light which it possesses. But in us is more than society can grasp, more than we can grasp. To know ourselves fully would be to know the universe. In the words of Emerson: "A man is a bundle of relations, a knot of roots, whose flower and fruitage is the world." But the world we live in is temporal as well as spatial. The fruitage is still to come. Little we realize what we are until we have been tested in the school of experience. "It doth not yet appear what we shall be." Most of our life is in the future, still to be created — by us and God.

Individual life is a series of metamorphoses. It is a drama in many acts. Shakespeare with his wonderful observation, and in the light of his day, dramatizes the course of a life:

> "All the world's a stage,
> And all the men and women merely players.
> They have their exits and their entrances;
> And one man in his time plays many parts,
> His acts being seven ages."

But there are more ages than even Shakespeare dreamed of, though we still understand very imperfectly the morphology of the soul. Conditions, too, have altered since Shakespeare's day; and we have succeeded in some respects, through our deeper knowledge of human nature, in making the stages more meaningful to the developing individual. Science may be able to head off the pitiable end that Shakespeare pictures. But the mysterious transformations of the soul remain the same. The awkward caterpillar emerges into the dreaming chrysalis until, for a little time, the butterfly tries its wings. Each stage seems to the developing individual the whole of life; but. to the maturer spectator each stage is both a life and a preparation for further living. The moments crowd upon each other in life's drama and hurry unconsciously to the further life beyond.

> "Like as the waves make towards the pebbled shore,
>   So do our minutes hasten to their end;
> Each changing place with that which goes before,
>   In sequent toil, all forwards do contend."

Always there is the same paradox: "We are more than we are;" and, because of the law inherent in our nature and in the process of the universe, "we are wiser than we know." Always there is the same illusion of self-sufficiency of each individual stage; always the same unconscious reaching forward into the unknown; always life speeds on to its creative future. Here let us tarry and build tabernacles says the healthy moment of joyous life.

> "How good is man's life; the mere living, how fit to employ
> All the heart and the soul and the senses forever in joy."

The tone in the symphony might feel the same, but it merges for its meaning into the larger whole. The child playing with its dolls feels that it is just itself, "just baby," but we see it as a moment in a creative life, developing according to an inner law. So each stage of life has its own centrism, its own illusion of sufficiency; but each in turn is transformed through unconscious processes into the next. Youth follows hard upon childhood with the romanticism and exaggeration, the undefined longing, the joy of living which are characteristic of youth. Its lessons, set by society, the school master, it gets because it must or to please its teachers, little mindful of the more serious obligations which await it. Maturity, with its responsibilities, the busy cares, the all absorbing tasks, comes all too soon. The poetry of youth fades into the common life of every day's routine. And maturity in turn by subtle and unnoticed changes passes into old age with the growing sense of the journey to that "undiscovered country from whose bourne no traveler returns."

Through the whole a wisdom wiser than ourselves guides our course while society is the mentor. In each stage, if we live according to our best instincts, we prepare best for the next. Each stage has a meaning and value all its own, and must not be treated as a mere preparation for the next. "To miss the joy is to miss all." To live merely for the future empties life of the significance that is. But each stage must hasten on to its larger destiny. To mother love, the child seems just the satisfaction of the mother instinct. She would fain keep it a child. But not even love can hold the new soul, once it has started on its journey. It is part of the destiny of humanity, the promise of the race. There is that about it which seems to say: "Wist ye not that I must be about my Father's business?" Life cannot tarry. It must ever respond to the call of the beyond.

> "Grow old along with me!
> The best is yet to be,
> The last of life, for which the first was made:
> Our times are in his hand
> Who saith, 'a whole I planned,
> Youth shows but half; trust God: see all, nor be afraid.' "

Life is a voyage of discovery. It is an adventure into an unknown world. And what do we discover? Something about things? Yes. But that is only incidental to our creative discovery of ourselves through human relations — a discovery of our capacities, limitations, and opportunities. In these human relations we find ourselves. Through the various crises of life, we discover, and others discover, what we are. The reminiscences consolidated in our nature come to light. There are ever fresh surprises as we meet new emergencies. Our hidden selfishness, our hidden nobility are brought out in the variety of social reactions. Our habits, our insights, our values are ever being reintegrated into a new pattern of personality. The process of education is not merely a discovery of a self already existing. It is a creative process. It is the function of the human mind to create. The impulse of life within us is ever striving to express itself. Within us is the instinct for wholeness, for consistency, for unity. Our various needs furnish the raw material, which the restless activity of thought must reconstruct into a meaningful whole. Habit and memory furnish the capacity of storage which enables the creative impulse to draw not only upon our own past experience, but upon the cumulative experience of the race, in building a more adequate future. There is within us the impulse of the artist to construct a whole, and personality is the product of the experimentation of this creative activity — first blindly, in a trial and error process, then more consciously in the light of the ideal within us. If we succeed in seizing upon the significant, then shall our lives become part of the creative process of history, the creative purpose of the ages. Else they become in turn raw material for further construction, clay in the hands of the Genius of the universe to make something better where He failed before.

The process of education is a process of disillusion. Things are not what we thought. We are not what we thought. The values of life change with the journey. What seemed important becomes unimportant. What seemed unreal becomes momentous. Life is always forward looking. Its ideal is always in the future. It is always striving for the beyond. In a sound healthy life, the ideal infinitely outstrips the attainment. The horizon ever moves forward with the journey. We always project our life into the future, even though the future is conceived as the mere fulfillment of our present wish. We little realize the future that is being created in our restless striving. But this

divine dissatisfaction with what we are is of the very essence
of life. It is the eternal Paradox: "We are more than we are."
We are part of a larger whole in creative participation with
which we must move onward or perish.

> "Ah, but a man's reach should exceed his grasp
> Or what's heaven for?"

But while we are thus hurrying forward in pursuit of our
destiny, there is always something lost. A glory has passed
away which cannot be had again. We cannot return to the
innocent laughter of childhood, to the unquestioning romance
of youth, once we have tasted of the tree of knowledge. As in
the old story of the Garden of Eden, the angel with the flaming
sword bars the way. The hands of time move not backward.
But with the losses there are compensations in the discovery
of our unknown potentialities, the genius of the soul. As of
old, man's disillusionment is his opportunity for a creative life,
for the reconstructing of circumstance in terms of a more
conscious ideal. Always there is the work to be done; for each
individual there is his unique creative vocation. The meaning
of this vocation, to be sure, changes with the ever widening
circles of social experience. We ever discover more exacting
standards of value. The excellence which we strive for seems
ever more unattainable, until it fades into the infinite perspective of the future. We discover ourselves as "unprofitable
servants" of the ideal. But do not be discouraged. In this larger
vision of life is salvation. Our life can be realized only in the
larger life of the race and of the universe. If we do our part
in loyalty to the whole; if we create in the light as we see the
light, we shall contribute even now in our unique measure to
the larger fulfillment, until the curtain opens in the presence
of God. The sense of disillusionment and failure is but the
initiation of true souls into the larger mysteries. For a man
with ideals and seriousness, "the best is yet to come." Let us
not waste time in vain regrets over the past. Regrets are useless

except as they result in a new zest for improvement. Ever the rainbow of hope and faith shall point the way to better things.

> "My heart leaps up when I behold
> A rainbow in the sky:
> So was it when my life began
> So is it now I am a man,
> So be it when I shall grow old
>   Or let me die!
> The child is father of the man:
> And I could wish my days to be
> Bound each to each by natural piety."

And if our best efforts seem to fail, let us remember that it is not so much what we do as what we would do, what we honestly and sincerely strive for, which matters. The rest lies with God. The password to each veil of the future is the same: Be loyal to the best that is in you and about you. Greater light will come by-and-by.

In this creative faith the individual soul can make its solitary venture without fear into that undiscovered country where the fog of death curtains off our life, for it is confident that no evil can happen to those who live for the best, whether in life or after death. One by one goes the eternal procession into the beyond, while love and hope stand gazing wistfully toward the realm where articulate communication fails, real though the spiritual bond remains. But whatever our lot, it cannot be that the universe made us for naught or that aught which we truly achieve is in vain. Through God's own purgatorial fires shall this bit of precious energy somehow be refined and start on its nobler destiny. In some way, God's own way, it shall play its part in God's universe. In some way, it shall share in harmonious activity and cooperation with the divine, if we are loyal to the best. What else matters? Destiny is not something ready-made and inevitable. It is not fate, but something we help to create.

CHAPTER FOURTEEN

HISTORIC DESTINY

"We are more than we are." We are woven into the historic destiny of the race as threads of tapestry. We are heirs to the faith of our fathers, the promise for which they toiled and died. And in turn, history is the expression of our efforts, our aspirations, our ideals. *Our* promise, too, our completion, like that of our fathers, lies in the future. While our life's train is moving, history on which we are carried is moving too. Here, also, we live in part; we cannot see the greater whole. At best our knowledge looks backward — it is like the perspective from the observation car of the moving train — while our hope and conduct necessarily carry forward; our faith strives to divine the unseen and uncreated reality of the future.

In the history of the race, as in individual life, the present moment, the present stage of life and insight, seems the whole of reality. It is always the present hopes and ideals we strive to complete. We look at the past through a glass coloured by our present meaning. We see the future as a projection of our present wish. It is human nature to be absorbed in its present tasks and struggles, to see the world from the point of view of its immediate needs. We can but dimly realize the cumulative past sacrifices which have made our life possible. Still less can we realize the fuller meaning of our efforts as these are taken up into the pattern of the future. Thus life is ever reaching out unconsciously into the beyond. "We are wiser than we know," by virtue of the organic law of the process of which we are part. Of every true and earnest individual or people it may be said: "He builded better than he knew." Even so, early man invented and struggled to meet his immediate needs. He

161

nurtured large families; he improved the crude tools of the past and invented better tools; he battled with nature and wild beasts and the selfish spirit of men. He lived true to his deeper instincts. He worked and struggled for his own — his own family, his own clan — to the best of his strength and insight. Little did he realize that he was the founder of civilization; that he made possible by his loyalty and efforts the inventions of the future, the art of the future, the larger social cooperation and ideals of the future.

Thus man, when true to his best, has ever built on the past; and has ever tried to reconstruct the past, to meet the immediate needs of his generation. And as he has built in loyalty to his best insight, he has added to the temple not made with hands, — the spiritual structure of humanity. Little did the handful of Greeks who fought at Marathon realize that their courage and bravery determined the course of Western civilization. They fought for their hearthstones, for the soil and institutions which they loved. The greater meaning of their conduct was hidden to them. Little could our forefathers, in the dark days of Valley Forge, realize the destiny which depended upon them. But through cold and hunger and raggedness and sacrifices of every sort, they remained loyal to the hope that was in them — the ideal of a self-determining people, creating their own institutions according to the light that was theirs, free from autocracy and despotism. But they did more than liberate a country; they gave a new impulse to democracy in their own Anglo-Saxon race and thus helped to make conscious its ideal of self-government for all. They lit a new light in oppressed France which it dramatized in a great revolution. They laid, in short, the foundations of a government built on justice and good will, however imperfectly we have realized the dream as yet. Little did the generation that passed through the Civil War realize the future import of their struggle and sacrifices that the Union might be saved. But they were loyal to their faith and to the vision of their great leader and fought the bitter struggle to the end. Little could they foresee the importance of a united nation in the great world struggle for democracy today. They fought for an America isolated from the world; but their loyal sacrifice made possible a new world factor in the upward struggle of humanity, if we remain loyal to our insight, as they were to theirs.

Thus have men worked and sacrificed in loyalty to their best. And always they have been wiser than they knew. Always they have builded unconsciously for the greater future. Always the promise of the race is in the beyond. In the words of the Biblical writer: "And these all, having obtained a good report through faith, received not the promise: God having provided some better thing for us, that they without us should not be made perfect." Neither shall we be made perfect excepting through the struggles and devotion of those that follow after us. Our relation to the future is like that of runners in a relay race. If we are sluggish and lazy, the future generations start handicapped. Their efforts depend upon our efforts. But so also do our efforts depend upon their success. If they fail through our handicap or their own lack of earnestness, our work, our life fails of that larger completion which must make our life significant. Both our tragedy and our success are an organic part of the future. We give hostages to the future in the shape of our own life with its net results. We place ourselves, our hopes, the Promise, in the keeping of the future, as the past with its aspirations placed itself in our keeping. What are our efforts without the efforts of those who follow us? In a sense it is true that "There is a Destiny which shapes our ends, rough hew them as we will." We are carried forward by something larger than ourselves. But we are a creative part of that Destiny. The promise of the race can only be realized by the devoted and honest sacrifices of the successive generations of history. Thus must we look forward and prepare ourselves for the nobler future, as the Hebrews looked forward to the coming of the Messiah. And the real coming of the Kingdom of Heaven is precisely this growth of insight and value in the succession of the ages.

Human history is the story of man's efforts to create a social environment suited to his evolving instincts and needs. It is a long experiment, full of tragic experience, in which man has discovered more and more the meaning of his life, his dependence on his fellows and the advantages of cooperation for a common weal. Thus the common bond in which man has found his vocation has ever been enlarged to meet man's needs. By means of his cumulative tradition man has been able to profit by his past successes and failures and thus to establish greater harmony of adjustment with his kind and with the universe. There has ever been bitter conflict between various types of ideals. In this conflict the capacity for cooperation has through the ages been increasingly victorious over narrow selfishness and clannishness. Selection has continually been at work to eliminate the unsocial individual and unsocial groups and to establish the ascendancy of the more social types. Thus the man of social instincts, of capacity for teamwork, is gradually becoming master of the earth. The predatory type must eventually pass, because of the lack of any permanent bond of coherency. It must crumble by its own weight, if not from conquest by the more social types. Good will and fair play have more strength than selfishness. "The meek shall inherit the earth."

The progress of civilization, however, has not been all gain. There have been losses as well as compensations. The man of tools and organization has too often played the part of Cain to his weaker, less equipped brother. But Abel's blood crieth to heaven and Cain wears in his soul the brand of his ruthless selfishness. We know now that there is much beauty in the culture and art of peoples who have been crowded to the wall — even those that we call primitive. We have come to feel, it is hoped, that it is our part to act as big brother to these peoples and to help them as best we may to realize their destiny — a destiny born out of their blood and tradition — and to protect them from unscrupulous exploitation, whether by individuals or nations. The superiority of the sword is a one-sided criterion at best and succumbs in the end to superiority of the spirit — the superiority of intelligence and good will. But in the meantime how much has perished by the vandalism of man that can never be repaired. The process of creating the beast, man, into the image of God is a long and costly one.

The end is not yet. It has ever been the illusion of human beings that the end has come with the consolidated insight of the age in which they live. Having established the gains of the past in customs and institutions, the mass feel so secure and comfortable in their entrenchments that they would rather fight on the defensive than venture forth on new conquests. The group is wise backwards. It ever discountenances the men of vision as rash and dangerous. Now, as of old, it builds the tombs of the prophets that are past and crucifies those that are sent. "Woe unto you Scribes and Pharisees, hypocrites! because ye build the tombs of the prophets, and garnish the sepulchres of the righteous." The instinct of self-preservation senses the crisis, even before the creator of new ideals does. It gives Socrates the hemlock and crucifies Jesus, because with their creative spirit, loyal though they mean to be, the present order cannot persist. To the mass, novelty means danger, conformity means safety. It cannot realize in its blindness that past attainments are but instruments, raw material, towards a larger creative destiny. The past furnishes us our tools and sets us our task, the present is our opportunity, not the goal to be stopped at.

> "The old order changeth, yielding place to new
> And God fulfills himself in many ways,
> Lest one good custom should corrupt the world."

It is ever thus. The new spirits must be tried out by braving the trenches of the established customs of the past, until the new ideals prove their superiority for practical living.

Tragedy, therefore, is of the very nature of progress. "I came not to bring peace but a sword," says the greatest pioneer in human history. No life, no progress, without vicarious sacrifice. The scarlet thread of pain runs through the whole process of development. Progress does not come by conventions and councils. They register the opinion of the past and the present. New insight is God's gift to the individual who catches the drift of the onward movement. Creativeness is forward looking. Its compensation is in the future. It must ever project itself anew into the unknown. It ever means risk and experiment. It means bitter conflict, and will ever mean so, until human nature at large develops an instinct of forward looking and becomes tolerant. The path of progress leads over Golgotha. It is significant that Golgotha has always had a double function, the place of execution of criminals and of prophets. Jesus was crucified between two thieves. The reason is that both are non-conformists; and in its blindness society cannot discriminate between what harkens back to the brute and what is prophetic of the kingdom of heaven. Hence Jesus prays: "Father, forgive them for they know not what they do." No gain without sacrifice; no victory without struggle and pain. But the great souls of history have made the sacrifice joyfully. It is not the pain that is significant. The criminals, crucified with Jesus, suffered more physical pain than he. They attended to the pain, he to the glory of the cause. It is the cause which makes the suffering redemptive.

The procession of humanity goes over Golgotha. From time to time millions are drafted by the vested rulers of this world as cannon fodder to satisfy their vanity and pride. But the sacrifice even of the unwilling millions shall not be in vain. They shall be disillusioned and redeemed through the suffering they are forced to undergo. Others, conscious of the ideal of human freedom, have laid down their lives willingly, in order that justice and kindness between man and man, and between group and group may triumph in the world. They did not live unto themselves, neither did they die unto themselves. In the great crises of life they have joyfully and eagerly thrown their whole weight on the side of God. What does it matter if life is longer or shorter, so it counts. A few moments in the turning of the tide of a great cause are worth infinitely more than a long life of comparative indifference. They have done and are doing their bit in the upward struggle of man. They are the hope of the ages. Humanity shall crown them with the laurel wreath that never fades.

The rank and file, the great army of toilers are lifting their faces to the light; they are acquiring discipline in the stern school of experience, they are learning the value of each other and their strength in cooperation, they are rising to a new consciousness of their common life. Comrades in toil and death, they are becoming conscious of their might and the days of their oppressors are numbered. They are discovering that organization can be made an instrument, instead of being a master; and they are learning to use not only industrial, but political organization for man, for human happiness. Through mistakes and suffering they are learning the meaning of the common good. Over Golgotha goes the procession of the future. Golgotha is the death of the past, the new birth, the raising of a new standard of value. In its sign of joyful and vicarious sacrifice shall humanity conquer.

Humanity must pass through its Lent of pain and sacrifice before its immortal hope can be realized. But after winter comes spring. After the festival of the Passion comes the festival of the Resurrection — not only one sacrifice and one resurrection, but every individual and age must learn to renounce in obedience to the larger life in order that it may experience the joy of deathless victory. Life and hope shall ever blossom anew in a soil made productive by the blood of humanity's heroes. In the agony of Gethsemane humanity shall hear, as never before, the voice of God, its better self, calling to creative effort for a larger ideal, a nobler future for the race.

The past organization of humanity is passing through a tremendous cataclysm. Like a mighty glacier which has torn loose from its moorings and is seeking a new equilibrium, or some earthquake re-establishing anew the earth's crust,

> "The chaos of a mighty world
> Is rounding into shape."

Certain it is that the old cleavages of tribalism and nationalism are too unstable to hold human life in its onward movement. A new equilibrium must be found, if peace and harmony are to rule. The gospel of the Golden Rule must become the conscious platform of humanity. This means not only a new equilibrium in our international relations; but it means first and foremost a new conception of our personal relations. For group relations must in the last analysis be the reflection of personal relations. It means that each man shall count for one in personal significance. It means that no one — man, woman or child — must be used as a mere instrument for the selfish ends of others. It means a new ideal of productiveness, the ideal of each one increasing the common fund of value according to the measure of his ability. It means a new joy in work and in friendly cooperation. It means that the old cleavages of classes must pass away in the new consciousness of man; that opportunity shall be universal; and that honor shall be bestowed for distinguished service to the whole. It means that we shall use the social resources for the social good, instead of the enhancement of predatory interests that tax society in order to debauch themselves in luxurious idleness. It means that the realization of humanity shall be the supreme concern of man.

The struggle is a long one. We have as yet won only the

front-line trenches. There is much labor, much sacrifice ahead, before the victory is won. But in the words of Abraham Lincoln: "Let us have faith that right makes might; and in that faith let us dare to do our duty as we understand it." We are not better than our fathers. As they sacrificed in faith that we might have greater opportunities, so must we in turn be willing to sacrifice for the larger humanity of the future, "with malice toward none, with charity for all, with firmness in the right, as God gives us to see the right." Only thus can there come to the world the brighter, fairer day for which the ages have toiled; only in creative devotion to the whole shall we find that peace which the world cannot give. In the triumphant song of George Sterling:

> "Be ye lift up, O everlasting gates
> Of that far city man shall build for man!
>   O fairer Day that waits,
> The splendor of whose dawn we shall not see
> When selfish bonds of family and clan
> Melt in the higher love that yet shall be!
> O state without a master or a slave,
>   Whose law of light we crave
> Ere morning widen on a world set free!"

CHAPTER FIFTEEN

COSMIC DESTINY

"We are more than we are." Our human striving and history is part of a larger cosmic order. While we are moving, the universe is moving too. The cosmos is an order of time, not a static order. Human nature itself is being slowly but surely changed in the process, in accordance with a cosmic law which we can but faintly grasp. The process of the universe is a genuinely creative process. In the creative interaction of the individual with the whole, there arise new structures, new levels of value. The present is not made merely of the whole cloth of the past; it is not the mere unraveling of its implications; it means the creating of new meanings and values as the larger destiny of the universe becomes incarnated into finite relations. We live in part, but through us and above us is the whole. This whole is itself constituted, so far as its concrete meaning is concerned, in the process. History is not the heaping up of blind accidents. There is a direction, a law which governs the process, as the old is transformed into the new. Evolution is an experiment in which the constructive Genius of the universe works out his infinite ideal in the flux of circumstance. So far as human evolution is concerned, this experimentation is two-fold — on the one hand, it is biological, the creating of a type, through variation and selection, which can yield a fuller, higher life; on the other hand, it is sociological, the creating of a tradition and institutions by means of which we can rise on our dead selves to higher selves, standing on the shoulders of the past and thus reaching upward into the future. Our life is thus organic to the whole of life and to the universe of which life is a part. But our life also contributes a new value to the whole. The whole is not a statuesque whole, but a growing, creative whole. It is a symphony of time.

In this conception of man's place, we are departing radically from the philosophy of a past century. Perhaps this philosophy has been nowhere more nobly expressed than in our own Emerson. According to Emerson the universe is eternally complete in one edition. There is no future, no history in the proper sense. "There is properly no history, only biography. . . . Civil history, natural history, the history of art and the history of literature — all must be explained from individual history, or must remain mere words. There is nothing but is related to us, nothing that does not interest us — kingdom, college, tree, horse, or iron shoe, the roots of all things are in man. . . . All inquiry into antiquity — all curiosity respecting the pyramids, the excavated cities, Stonehenge, the Ohio Circles, Mexico, Memphis, is the desire to do away this wild, savage and preposterous There and Then, and introduce in its place the Here and Now. It is to banish the me and supply the not-me." The reason is that for Emerson there is but "one mind common to all individual men. Every man is the inlet to the same and to all of the same." All that is necessary then is to know our own mind and we know the universe.

Emerson's philosophy voices the tendency of the 19th century — the self-sufficiency of the individual. But there is more to human life than separate individuals; there is the common bond within which they must find their meaning and vocation; and without which they would be mere abstractions. And there is the creative destiny of the race. History is more than biography, as the organism is more than cells. There is the organic life of a temporal whole — a whole in the making. In it the individual himself is in the process of creation. It is not yet clear what man shall be; but new instincts and capacities must be developed if the social bond is to be made perfect.

The universe in short is a creative process in which things

really happen, in which the mind of man is itself being made, with instincts which will telescope into other minds, present and future, in a creative society. In the words of Browning:

> "Progress is
> The law of life; man is not man as yet."

We are not like the old pictures in Florence:

> "They are perfect; how else? —
> They shall never change;
> We are faulty; why not? —
> We have time in store."

It is this creative character of the process which makes it so difficult to comprehend life. We can only understand the present in the light of the future; and the future we can understand only when it is made. "Behold I make all things new," says the Spirit of history. The Genius of the whole is ever embodied in new forms and thus comes to have new meaning. There are no static types, but the types themselves of life and of institutions are being made in the creative process and persist only until the Spirit of history expresses itself in more perfect types. Always we are haunted by a sense of imperfection, with the sense of the greater beyond. But the perfection is infinite, while our striving is finite. It is a dynamic perfection. We must ever move forward or die. In the drama of life,

> "Nothing is
> But what is not,"

though the "what is not" is continuous with what is, the prospective incarnation of the same law of development. Life must ever be what is not, but ought to be. It must find its end and joy in achievement.

We are part of the organic unity of cosmic history. In our blood are the reminiscences — stored we know not how — of the whole past story of evolution, the long genealogy from the primitive forms, the reminiscences of the cosmic weather that we have passed through. The past tugs at our coat tails and would fain drag us back whence we came. Ever and again we lapse into the primitive, only more brutal because more sophisticated. Our cannibal nature crunches its fellow beings in the jaws of war, glorying in destruction; or we forget in our personal relations that we are our brother's brother and lapse to the state of Cain.

Savage, cave man, back to Pithecanthropus — all that is but recent history. The genealogical tree goes back, in its obscure transitions, through mammals, pre-mammals, reptiles, amphibians, fishes, invertebrates, protozoa, bacteria to the primordial basis of life — hundreds of millions of years. Then what? We stand before a new mystery, nature's creative synthesis of life from what we, in our ignorance, call lifeless elements — a synthesis ever repeated in the creative process that transmutes what we call matter into life, in the economy of nature. And then? What is the meaning of the long story, of this series of cumulative adaptive variations, with their anticipations of the future? What is the significance of the selection through which nature rectifies her guesses in the long experiment? Somehow there is the constructive law of the whole — the temporal architecture of the universe. As life progresses in its adaptations, it gradually evolves organs to sense, however dimly, the direction in which it is moving — those higher instincts which point to a creative whole of unity and beauty, and at length develops the capacity to reflect, however inadequately, upon the principles that are immanent in its history from the outset. We have been too prone to regard the primitive instincts as the key to reality and to doubt the testimony of the later ideal instincts. But the latter are precisely the inspiration of the whole from which we have sprung, the urge towards the future of which we are a part. It is the order of the universe which rises to dim apprehension in us. It is the 'recollection' of God who is our home, our destiny, and who, in the travail of the cosmos, tries to bring to birth in us the consciousness of Himself. It is this immanent creative Spirit which sets the trend of the cosmic process. "For the earnest expectation of the creature waiteth for the manifestation of the sons of God."

We must not imagine that we are the stopping place of God's creativeness. Here too there is the illusion in human nature which makes it feel that the present stage is the last stage; that the climax has come with us. In the meantime we are carried on with the current of the greater life to a destiny which we cannot see. Present man is but a transition, a passing stage in the evolution of life. He is a link between the ape man and the greater humanity to come.

In a lucid moment this idea was expressed in an immortal way by Nietzsche:

"I teach you the superman. The man is something who shall be overcome. What have you done to overcome him?

All being before this made something beyond itself, and you will be the ebb of this great flood, and rather go back to the beast than overcome the man?

What is the ape to the man? A mockery or painful shame. And even so shall man be to the superman: a mockery, or a painful shame.

Man is a chord, tied between beast and superman — a chord above an abyss.

A perilous arriving, a perilous traveling, a perilous going backward, a perilous trembling and standing still.

What is great in man is that he is a bridge, and no goal; what can be loved in man is that he is a going over and a going under.

I love them that know not how to live, be it even as those going under, for such are those going across.

I love them that are great in scorn, because they are they that are great in reverence, and arrows longing toward the shore."

If the last five hundred thousand years have produced modifications which have transformed man from something like an anthropoid ape to what we know as man today, what reason is there to suppose that the changes have stopped now? It is true that the exterior of man, his gross anatomy, seems to have undergone only slight changes, according to the evidence of discovered remains, during some twenty thousand years; but his finer structures, the subtle connections in his brain, his mental capacities, making possible his increasingly complex adjustments and his capacity for a nobler soul, must have changed greatly during that time; and the process of variation and of social selection has never been more marked than now. Nor can we say that the present changes are merely in the social environment — man's tradition and education. It is true that human nature changes but slowly, while social heredity may increase in geometric progression; and a great deal of the progress today must be credited primarily to a change in the social environment. But without the modification of individual human nature — through the arising of new instincts, new capacities for imagination and appreciation — the external framework of society, in the way of laws and institutions, will be futile in producing a better order of things. If we are to have a higher society, human nature must undergo still further modifications in the line of conscientiousness in the performance of common duties, of devotion to the common bond with man and the universe. While man retains his selfish and predatory nature, peace will be but a truce in the ever-recurring conflict, nowithstanding all treaties and agreements. You cannot make man love his neighbor as himself by external agreements or compulsions. No mere increase of material comfort is going to make men content. Mere prudence will be unequal in the future, as it is at present, to restrain men or groups in their insatiable thirst for power.

It doth not yet appear what we shall be in the long aeons of time. We can only project our ideals of the present into the future. It is certain that we cannot overcome our present limitations through merely individual striving. Nietzsche's dominating egoist is a glorification of nineteenth century individualism — he is not a prophecy of the future. The real superman, the greater man of the future, is not an unscrupulous individualist, crushing others to attain his own. Such a type would make society impossible and would mean a return to the jungle. The greater man we look for is an individual who through his greater capacity for love and his greater capacity of imagination is able more truly and helpfully to share the life of others. He will strive for excellence that he may serve his fellows, that he may enrich the life of friendship. He will strive to be a son of God that he may be more truly a son of man. We can discover our individual destiny only when we make the most of our capacities in a common life. The whole trend of human evolution has been in the direction of give and take, of the recognition of mutual dependence and mutual aid.

There has been in the past too great a tendency to apotheosize efficiency. More efficient man must become; he must attain greater mastery of the forces of nature; he must improve the human organization until it works with the greatest economy. But there always remains the question: Efficiency for what? Man must not be made merely a means in the struggle for existence, whether individual or corporate. Man has not only the right to work; but the right to appreciate, the right to love, the right to friendship in creativeness.

If our destiny cannot be that of egoistic individualism, seeking merely its own, neither can it be communistic socialism, such as the life of the bee, which has merged the individual in the hive. While it has perfected a wonderful organization at which we marvel, it has sacrificed plasticity and progress in its extreme emphasis on the life of the group. Organization there must indeed be, to make progress possible. But it must be cooperative organization — organization in which the individuality, initiative and excellence of the part is furthered in the common bond. For the light of eternity must shine on the race through individual insight; creativeness must be individual creativeness, however much encouraged and furthered by the opportunities of the community. A nobler society is possible only by the creation of nobler individuals. Not the individual alone nor social organization alone, but individuals finding their opportunity and incentive in a common life and a common life enriched by the creativeness of free individuals — that seems to be the only workable ideal of humanity.

The test of progress, so far as we can see, must be the greater capacity for human relations — for justice, for kindness, for friendship. How pusillanimous and petty to live for individual pleasure or self-realization in the light of such a destiny! Progress has been made by those whose instinct has led them to live for a larger whole, whose life reached out into the future to grasp the promise of the race — the promise to Israel, the promise to Greece, the promise to Rome, the promise to France, the promise to England, the promise to America, but above all the promise to humanity. Glory to those who sacrifice for the future, who respond to the instinct to battle against the shackles of the past that would hold us, who work that a nobler type may prevail — a type of creative helpfulness. This is indeed the type of the Nazarene: "Ye know that they which are accounted to rule over the Gentiles exercise lordship over them; and their great ones exercise authority upon them. But so shall it not be among you: but whosoever will be great among you, shall be your minister: And whosoever of you will be the chiefest, shall be servant of all. For even the Son of Man came not to be ministered unto, but to minister, and to give his life a ransom for many." This is the gospel of genuine democracy.

Our social structure has been built in the main upon two instincts — the passion for power and the passion for property. The select and unscrupulous few have striven to dominate the mass and to acquire possession of the earth, so as to make the mass work for them while they enjoyed a life of leisure. Work has been regarded as the function of slaves while leisure and dominion over others have been genteel. But the old crust is breaking, the masses are in revolt. Pursuant of the ideals of their former masters, the masses have sometimes turned the tables. Having come into power, they have exploited the few and made them do the menial work. The logic holds so far as the old order is concerned, namely, that those who hold the power shall make the others their beasts of burden. The many have just as much right to exploit the few as the few the many. But practically the logic breaks down, because there are not enough of the few to do the work for the masses. The trouble is with the whole ideal of power and exploitation. At best the instincts for dominion and possession are insatiable and so cannot bring happiness. The more power or the more wealth a man gets, the more he wants in proportion. But the old ideal is fundamentally wrong. It degrades those who pursue it, as well as those who are the victims of it, into mere instruments. It sacrifices humanity to soulless idols. The new social order must be built on a new foundation. And the only ideal that can eventually work is the gospel of Jesus — the golden rule, the ideal of mutual service and mutual helpfulness in a common enhancement of life, in short an ideal of friendship built upon genuine personal relations. This is the only ideal that will work, because it is the only ideal that is right. It is as wrong for one class to dominate and enslave, as it is for another. The true ideal is cooperation for the common bond, for mutual improvement and happiness — losing one's self that one may find one's self. This must be the ideal of the future for individuals and nations alike, if humanity is to survive. We must learn to reverence humanity in ourselves and others, even if the latter be separated from us by national or racial boundaries. Work must be emancipated from its menial past, and glorified into creative cooperation for a common welfare. In the inspired words of Robert Burns,

"Then let us pray that come it may,
   (As come it will for a' that)
That sense and worth, o'er a' the earth,
   May bear the gree and a' that.
      For a' that, and a' that —
   It's comin yet, for a' that,
   When man to man, the world o'er,
   Shall brithers be for a' that."

When suffused with this higher light of progress — the light of love and sympathy, of creative participation in a common life — we shall indeed become citizens of the world; we shall understand past ages better because we shall be conscious of sharing their creative mission. Through sympathetic insight we shall be able in a measure to bridge the gulf between our own age and earlier ages, both in our individual life and in social history. We shall be able to enter into the creative mission, not only of Israel, Greece, and Rome, but also of the more primitive peoples who labored more wisely than they knew, in building the foundations of our social structure. In this way, we shall attain better understanding of our relation to the larger drama of life with its cumulative struggle, its vicarious sacrifice. In the realizing of our creative vocation, we shall use science as an instrument to control our bodies and our environment for sound living, at the same time that we rise, through a larger knowledge of nature, and of human nature as showing the potentiality of nature, to an appreciation of nature's direction. Art shall become the interpretation of the common joy in creativeness, instead of the titillation of an aristocratic caste; and religion shall become our devotion to the common good — to the spirit that inspires the best in the universe. We shall thus be led to greater sympathy and cooperation with the creative Genius of the whole. Of this greater humanity of the future we may indeed use the eloquent words of Jean Leon Jaurès: "They will have a better understanding of the hidden meaning of life, whose mysterious aim is the harmony of all consciences, of all forces, and of all liberties. They will understand history better, and will love it, because it will be their history, since they are the heirs of the whole human race. Finally, they will understand the universe better; because, when they see conscience and spirit triumphing in humanity, they will be quick to feel that this universe which has given birth to humanity cannot be fundamentally brutal and blind; that there is spirit everywhere, soul everywhere, and that the universe itself is simply an immense confused aspiration toward order, beauty, freedom, and goodness. Their point of view will be changed; they will look with new eyes, not only at their brother men, but at the earth, and the sky, rocks, and trees, animals, flowers, and stars."

How shall we prepare for this larger future? In this infinite universe how shall we mortals of a day find our way? We may well exclaim: "O Lord thy world is so great, and we are so small, have mercy upon us." Our insight is indeed limited. We can see the universe only in terms of our experience. And there is ever the law of relativity in our human sphere, as the past is re-created into the present and the present into the future. History is always in transition, always being transformed into something new. The changes may be too slow for us to notice or they may overwhelm us with their catastrophes. But change is of the very nature of things; and with time the perspective changes, the standard changes. Only the law of the whole runs like a silver thread through it all; and that law we can only dimly grasp, for it runs into the future. But always we must be sincere; always we must act in accordance with our best insight; always we must give our entire energy to the cause of truth as we can see it; always we must be devoted in piety to the spirit of the whole, to the promise of the future. Always we must dare to interpret the world afresh, to reconstruct the past and its formulae, in terms of our present insight. Always we must strive to be masters of ourselves and our environment

— we must teach with the authority that is in us, not as slaves of the past. Always we must trust our soul and its intimations. We must walk in the light as God gives us to see the light. A glory has passed; we must create a new glory.

> "Heartily know
> When half-gods go,
> The gods arrive."

But half-gods are better than no gods; we must ever be willing to make use of the wisdom of the past in steering towards the uncharted seas of the future, as we must be willing to remake the chart in accordance with the light that is given us.

Our knowledge lightens up the past; and by indicating the wake in which our ship has traveled helps us to move towards the future. At best life is a venture of faith. We live in part, and therefore we can know only in part. "Meantime within man is the soul of the whole" — the cosmic destiny of which he is a part. There is, I believe, an instinct which guides us, when we honestly and thoughtfully listen to it. Should the bee have an instinct for the future and man have no guidance in his far more complex destiny? Should the migratory birds have an instinct to find their way, when stimulated by cold and wind, to the Southland, and we be lost in the cosmos? Always there is the call of the whole, "the last of life for which the first was made;" there is somehow a homing instinct in human nature — "to God who is our home." In the meantime, we must live by faith, even as our fathers did.

Faith must ever precede reason. But this does not mean the abandonment of reason. Reason must judge between faiths. It must correlate our faiths into a philosophy of the world. That the world is a mad whirl of chance, or that it is a creative order working towards goodness and beauty, either is a faith. The question is which is the more reasonable. Faith without reason is blind, reason without faith is empty. Faith is the life blood of reason, reason is the eyes of faith. Faith has its roots in our instinctive nature; it is an intimation of the universe of which we are a part; it feels its way into the darkness of the future. Reason follows with a lantern. It inspects and examines the paths and removes the underbush. It criticises, simplifies and makes consistent our faiths. Faith furnishes the premises of life. Reason organizes faith into a conscious purpose and scrutinizes its working in the emergencies of life.

Reason in its true meaning is not opposed to faith; it is faith striving to become conscious of its meaning; it is faith creating in the light instead of in the dark; it is but good sense. If it is true that we must believe in order to understand, it is also true that we must consciously try out our beliefs. Otherwise our beliefs are all leveled to the same plane; and one belief has no claim over another. We sink into the darkness of undiscriminating superstition. We must ever hold that the universe is at bottom a reasonable universe. As we must believe that the great Mind of the universe is carrying on intelligent and creative experimentation in the universe as a whole, so must we in our small way carry on intelligent experimentation within our experience in order that the great experiment of the ages may be shared by us and furthered by us. We must have faith in thought, even though in us it can illumine the pathway only in part. We must believe that the forces of the spirit are stronger than any material forces; "that thoughts rule the world." We must believe that there is a kinship of our best — our noblest thought and striving — with the Genius of the universe. In our ideal creativeness and the faith which is its inspiration, we are in a small measure architects with God of the universe — builders of the nobler temple of the future. Out of the gradual increments of our thought and sacrifice shall grow the infinitely nobler structure, as the coral builds the islands of the sea.

Life is a venture, a risk. But we are not without guidance. We have the experiments of the past — the slow-working experiments of nature in evolving a new world of which we are part and in which we too shall be passed. We have also the experiments of creative intelligence which indeed is part of the cosmic process, but which can be made to yield more rapid results of control and appreciation when it becomes conscious of itself in the human mind. The great experiment of the ages is only within very small limits within our control. We are part of it and we can know it only dimly. But there is within us, and beyond us, the law of the whole, striving to become incarnate, which we can bring to somewhat clearer and more effective, even if only temporary, expression. The progress of life will require ever new and more adequate editions. These can come only if we utilize the creative intelligence that is ours in reconstructing the present environment in devotion to the larger whole.

O for the capacity to enter into this larger life of the universe; to feel the harmony of the spheres, the symphony of worlds, with its dur and moll, its major and minor keys; to become conscious of the whole pattern of creative thought, its cadences in the arising and passing of worlds; to feel the greater bond of the universe — a bond of creative love — as God feels it, as future man we may believe shall feel it; to enter into communion with the invisible, with the noble saints of all the worlds; but in the present stage of development we must be loyal to our partial insight, realizing that at best our thought is but a poor prophecy of the greater future. But we may feel with Walt Whitman:

"Beautiful World of new, superber Birth, that rises to my eyes,
Like a limitless golden cloud, filling the western sky,
Thou Wonder World, yet undefined, unformed — neither do I define thee;
How can I pierce the impenetrable blank of the future?
I feel thy ominous greatness, evil as well as good,
I watch thee advancing, absorbing the present, transcending the past;

I saw thy light lighting and thy shadow shadowing, as if the entire
    globe;
But I do not undertake to define thee — hardly to comprehend thee;
I but thee name — thee prophecy, — as now!''

The religion of the past has been too much a passive religion
— a passive dependence on God, a passive resignation to things
as they are. It has been an attitude of letting God do it. The
religion we must proclaim for the future is the religion of the
creative life, the religion of doing our best in order that better
things may come, a religion of copartnership with the constructive Genius of the universe. There is a world in the process of
being created, a whole to be made, and we must help make it.
The impious man is the slacker, the idler, the man who fails
to do his part. The pious man is the productive man, the man
who strives for excellence in creative comradeship with men.
The kingdom of heaven is indeed at hand — it is within us,
though infinitely beyond us, waiting for expression in a larger
and nobler life. We worship God best when we work for
the best.

The religion of the future means that we must be devoted
above all to the cause — not of individual happiness or realization — but the realization of a greater humanity, with the
discipline and sacrifice which this implies. It means the rearing
in faith of a posterity, both physical and spiritual, which may
rise to an infinitely larger measure than ourselves. To this end
families must be raised in the fear of God and the hope of the
promise. For if the race comes to an end, or the best stock
comes to an end, the promise of the ages cannot come — not
on this earth. In other parts of the universe and through the
ages, God carries on infinite other experiments, in the hope of
somewhere realizing the best. If we fail through our selfishness and stupidity to attain the higher mission of the race,
other planets in other parts of the universe will prove the
potentialities of nature. But it is our business to try to make

the experiment succeed on this planet. Aside from making the loving sacrifice that the race may go on and that the law of life may thus realize itself in higher types, we must conscientiously strive and honestly cooperate that the future race may have the best spiritual environment that we can create. For without the proper spiritual heredity, the best physical heredity cannot avail. The religion of the future means in short the passionate love of the whole of life — of the ongoing of love and creativeness — that our little lives and efforts may not be in vain. We must realize our organic unity with all of life — life that precedes and life that follows after, and our creative destiny as part of this stream of life within the guidance of the whole. It is not a question of you or me, but of our creative contribution to the common bond, to the whole, each through each and all in all, in peace, love, and unity.

It is not in our power to picture the greater man of the future. He must be the gift of the universe in the fullness of time. But neither can he come without our cooperation. If we are loyal to our vocation; if we make our own the heritage of the past and in turn add our creative increment; if we hand down not only an improved tradition but sound blood that can carry the destiny of the race forward; if we in short prepare for the future in the true spirit of devotion to the best, then we may believe that the higher type shall come, in the creative destiny of which we are a part but which is greater than we. We shall not see the promised land but we are part of the procession in the historic life of the whole, and this may well be the realization of the promise.

The religion of the future is, like the religion of the past, a religion of the Promise, — the promise of the greater life to come, — though we may hope that we shall more consciously and, therefore, more adequately enter into the creative plan. Our destiny is indeed a high destiny. "Now are we the sons of God, but it doth not yet appear what we shall be." There is a larger kingdom of heaven to be created. If we work and sacrifice for the future in faith and intelligence, God's creative grace will make the promise real. To those who thus make themselves part of the divine creative purpose, the psalmist does not hesitate to apply the sublime term of gods: "I said Ye are Gods; and children of the most High." And who would begrudge the title son of God to the spiritual leader of the race: "Is it not written in your law, I said, Ye are gods? If ye call them gods unto whom the word came, and the scripture cannot be broken; say ye of him whom the Father hath sanctified, and sent into the world, Thou blasphemest; because I said I am the son of God." In him, the Nazarene, we find indeed the prophecy of the greater humanity, the incarnation of the promise of the future. No one was better aware than he of the law of creative continuity which passes our finite embodiments: "Greater works than these shall ye do, for I go to the Father."

The old order changeth. A new order is coming — an order of larger cooperation in the creative life. We must be loyal to the hopes and sacrifices of our fathers; we must accept with gratitude their heritage, working as they in faith for the greater promise. We must not squander nor neglect the treasure which we have received. But we must use it constructively, to re-create and enhance it, to add our bit; and facing toward the future we must ever work and wait for the greater day, the year of the Lord, the richer fulfillment of the promise of the ages. Let whatsoever is mean and unworthy pass away. Let whatever is good and noble be resurrected into a fuller day. Always there is the creative life of God working in and through us, as we are prepared for it and cooperate with it. And it is because of this larger life within us that we feel, in a day of struggle and sacrifice, a new devotion to the whole, — the emergence of the human soul from its instinctive chrysalis into a nobler and more glorious purpose.

EPILOGUE

The Spirit moves over the depths of space and through the abysms of time. To one looking at the universe as a collection of things in space, it might well appear to be chaos. But if we grasp the universe as an order in time, it becomes drama. There is rhythm and measure everywhere in the small and in the large. The energy of matter condenses into definite units and in return dissolves into the measured pulsations of radiation. There is evidence of architecture everywhere. The same atomic structures are repeated everywhere in space in the seasons of the cosmos; and so, we may be sure, are the more complex structures, as the climate permits — even as in our little part of the world. Everywhere the universe is open to thought as we become prepared. Everywhere the genius of nature works for harmony in the ages, though the material sets limitations. The willingness of the individual is a condition with which the Spirit of the universe must deal. It holds throughout that many are called but few are chosen. But those that lend themselves to the constructive genius of spirit go on to greater and greater perfection. The rest become raw material and framework for the creative advance of nature.

Everywhere there is rhythm and drama. The galaxies have a long span. But they too are measured and run a definite course of differentiation and dissolution. They are the clocks of the cosmic years. Within them are the condensations of stars, the great furnaces of cosmic energy that dissolve as radiation in their seasons. Around some of these stars are the satellites, the offspring, somehow, of stars and running their course within the larger system. They may seem obscure beside the brilliant parent, but it is in these that the parent becomes significant drama. For it is within the history of these fragments of stars that life appears and at length mind which can survey the course that nature travels and peer into its mysteries. Do I seem small and insignificant compared to the vast material world? What is the whole world of matter compared to thought?

It is spirit that runs through the cosmic ages and in its own providence guides the cosmic order to the birth of spirit. It is for this that the genius of spirit works and suffers through the ages — to be understood, to be appreciated. Nothing great can be attained except through work and suffering. It is a long and arduous experiment to bring spirit to birth. It means the framing of a body that can become the organ of life — equipped to respond to the rhythms of sound and colour and sweetness and fragrance that make a delightful world —, and that can store up the fruits of the struggle of life and transmit them to future generations. It means the building of a soul that, through habit and memory, can learn by living. It means creating the power of imagination to paint vistas of the future, it means the power of thought to arrive at understanding and control. It means the power of sympathy to live into, and feel at one with, the beauty and meaning of the world. It means the communion with other minds and best of all with the divine Spirit that stirs in the depths of our being and in the vast world about us, for it is spirit that binds the parts together into a drama of time and space.

It is an infinite privilege to be born into the world of spirit even for an instant, to wake even in a small way to the beauty and meaning of the world, yea, to the beauty and meaning of God. I thank God that I can share with Him in the enjoyment of His work, and that as creative mind, with my fellowminds, I can share in the creation of a new world, and help, as my strength goes, to bring order into chaos within me and about me. If it is only for a brief moment, I would not give it for all the aeons of stars and galaxies, for these are after all only the preparation and the frame for such a moment of living with God. I shall not fear the vast cosmic expanses, for the spirit of God pervades all space. And I shall not mourn my brief moment in the ages of time, for God is working, constructing and redeeming throughout all time. Wherever I am and whenever I am, I am with God and His love sufficeth. He has not brought me here and now for naught. My destiny is in Him and that is enough for me.